MASTER YOUR

Thesis

Proven strategies and methods:

It's time to get your life back!

ENDORSEMENTS

You are about to embark on the exciting, but daunting and anxiety-invoking, journey of postgraduate research, culminating in a thesis. Make the upfront investment to capacitate yourself fully and thoroughly for the journey by working through this practical guide on mastering this high-risk journey with its multitude of potential derailers. It will truly be worth your while by significantly enhancing your chances of not only reaching your destination successfully, but also in one piece personally.

Theo H. Veldsman, Former HOD: Department of Industrial Psychology and People Management, University of Johannesburg; Visiting and Extra-ordinary Professor at the University of Johannesburg and Stellenbosch Business School (USB) respectively; doctoral student study leader

As a supervisor and mentor of many postgraduate students, I found this book to be very practical and focused on the key aspects that you will come across in your journey of developing a thesis. Most postgraduate students are in a corporate environment and the majority of their writing on a daily basis is reports, which makes academic writing a challenge when they commence with the process of writing a thesis. The book starts by discussing your relationship with your supervisor, which is so important as you need that mentoring and guidance when going through this process for the first time. Planning is also very important; I always emphasise to students that if you plan your study and process in detail, you have half the work done. Project management is key to creating the discipline needed to write a successful thesis.

Prof. Adri Drotskie, Director: School of Management, University of Johannesburg; supervisor; mentor

This book is an engaging and compelling MUST read for anyone involved in writing research proposals and thesis writing. It is more than an indispensable step-by-step guide – it is energising, empathetic, motivational and authentic in navigating thesis writers through the very real emotional complexities that inevitably pop up during the course of writing a thesis. The call to "get your life back" differentiates this book from other thesis guideline publications that are currently in play. A huge thank you to the author who is a thesis coach, for an illuminating, brave and bold read, based on proven strategies, wisdom and insight that she has tried and tested over many years. For academic supervisors and for students, this book provides very valuable tips and tools to ace your thesis.

Dr. Shirley Zinn, Chair and Independent Non-Executive Director of Boards: Sanlam, MTN (SA), VNA and Spur Corporation

At 08h30 on Saturday 26 February 2022, at my invitation, Caroline Dale gave a two-hour virtual masterclass to almost 100 MBA treatise students on thesis writing. I personally attended one hour of the masterclass and confirm that it was of significant value to those who attended. Many attendees were of the view that this masterclass should be compulsory when students first enrol for a postgraduate degree. Caroline's first book is a comprehensive explanation of The Dale Method, her unique methodology to overcoming academic and thesis challenges. She includes a summary of the well-known psychological challenges and how to navigate them on any academic journey.

In my opinion, this book is an essential introduction for all postgraduate students who are obliged to write a thesis to graduate.

Dr Sam February, HOD: Nelson Mandela University Business School, Port Elizabeth

During August 2019, I was six weeks away from the deadline date for the submission of my dissertation, which involved research into the digitisation and technological change in the residential real estate industry of Oxford, UK (Oxford Brookes University).

I had hit a brick wall, my supervisor was away and inaccessible, and I was severely stressed. I needed help. My grandfather (through a good friend) suggested I review Caroline's website (The Thesis Coach). I found that Caroline specialised in coaching postgraduate students through the thesis process and I found her testimonials to be incredible.

The rest is history. I contacted Caroline and after bi-weekly intensive online sessions, many late night WhatsApp messages, daily communication, and a good dose of strict discipline and focus, I managed to submit my thesis on time and I achieved a distinction.

I strongly recommend Caroline and this book to anyone facing the challenges of submitting a good thesis on time.

Daniel Kramer, MSC Science (Business Management)

A much-needed contribution to the 'how-to' field of research writing, this approach by Caroline Dale is as humane and accessible as it is professional and thorough. From step-by-step guidelines on the components of a thesis framework to tips for managing self-doubt, exhaustion, stress and procrastination, the student about to embark on this challenging journey will be well-supported. As a lecturer and supervisor of postgraduate students, I have no hesitation in recommending this book. It is clear that this compassionate and strongly encouraging approach to completing a thesis is grounded in the author's own experience and that of her many satisfied clients. Embarking on completing a postgraduate thesis can be all-consuming, but with the help of Caroline Dale's book, you can succeed – and get your life back.

Dr Dorrian Aiken, lecturer in coaching and leadership development, Time to Think coach and consultant, Integral Master coach, COMENSA Master Practitioner

Caroline and I undertook our MPhil journey at the same time. She was an inspiration in the way that she drew together her skills in software and systems development and applied a process background to write a personal and profound thesis. As a member of her study group, I was an early reader of her thesis and was deeply impressed by the lyricism of her academic writing and her ability to excavate her personal experience against a background of research. We both delivered our theses in the shortest possible time; if I had not had Caroline to support me in person, I would have wanted this book.

Master your thesis – Proven strategies and methods: It's time to get your life back! contains wise and practical advice, drawn from both Caroline's experience and some of the best literature in the field of leadership of self and performance management. A unique book that addresses one of the biggest challenges in academia: how to support students through the thesis writing process. If you are doing a master's, or indeed any degree requiring a thesis, this book will be your secret recipe for success.

Sarah Arnot, Author, Executive Coach, Leadership Expert

Having been on the thesis journey three times, I have full empathy for what students go through embarking on this process! It can be daunting and often students are left to their own devices to "figure things out and find that golden thread", particularly at the postgraduate level. I have walked this journey with many a student as their supervisor for MBA research and can honestly attest first-hand to the level of support that is actually needed to demystify the elusive research process and to make a success of your thesis.

This book is a wonderful resource and handbook on taking master and doctoral level students through the process step-by-step with sound guidance and support that works alongside the guidance from your supervisor. The book leaves you with little gems that you are often not told about, but can make a world of a difference to your research experience. It is also a practical and user-friendly read; it is particularly helpful that the book breaks down and provides insight into every stage of the research process in a very structured way. What is most enlightening is that it offers students the opportunity to enjoy the elusive research process, reduce the anxiety and enable a platform of true learning and deep insights to take place!

Navlika Ratangee, Managing Director: ICAS Southern Africa; clinical psychologist; MBA graduate; MBA mentor; research supervisor; examiner

This book is written in plain language. It is easy to follow and drops the jargon. Not only will it help students, but it will help supervisors help students too. I have supervised 15 PhDs and 83 Master's students, and I wish that this book had been available much sooner. You absolutely nailed it with "Access to data" and "Simplicity is the key". Well done Caroline. Time for your PhD...

Prof. Mark Bussin, Chairperson: 21st Century (Pty) Ltd; consultant; author; professor; commissioner; non-executive director; pilot

This book will fill a large gap in the area of thesis development. An interesting, informative and logical practical roadmap is provided which addresses all elements and aspects of postgraduate study. This map will guide students not only to master the whole process, but also to deal with psychological challenges and health problems. The author's business experience, combined with evidence-based theories, makes for a compelling read, yet it is still easy to understand, practical and fun. This is a must-read for all students involved with postgraduate research studies.

Ebben S. van Zyl, Emeritus Professor: Department of Industrial Psychology, University of the Free State

First published in 2022.

ISBN: 978-1-86922-938-2 (Printed)
eISBN: 978-1-86922-939-9 (PDF eBook)

Published by KR Publishing
Republic of South Africa
Tel: (011) 706-6009
E-mail: orders@knowres.co.za
Website: www.kr.co.za

Typesetting, layout and design: Cia Joubert, cia@knowres.co.za
Cover design: Marlene de'Lorme, marlene@knowres.co.za
Infographics: Cherice Torr, cherice@livingoutthebox.co.za
Editing and proofreading: Jennifer Renton, jenniferrenton@live.co.za
Project management: Cia Joubert, cia@knowres.co.za

MASTER YOUR

Thesis

Proven strategies and methods:

It's time to get your life back!

CAROLINE DALE

kr
publishing

THE
DALE
METHOD

2022

For my clients: past, present and future.

TABLE OF CONTENTS

ABOUT THE AUTHOR

Caroline Yvonne Dale is the founder and CEO of The Thesis Coach (Pty) Limited, which was established in March 2018. She motivates, coaches and mentors postgraduate students towards graduation. Caroline's coaching is based on qualifications, experience, evidence-based theories, and first-hand knowledge of the psychological and technical challenges to submitting a top-class thesis on time. Her results are supported by extensive client testimonials.

Caroline's career spans more than 35 years, during which she enjoyed a successful 20-year career in stockbroking, almost entirely in information technology and project management. During preparation for her own thesis, for which she achieved a distinction, Caroline became aware of the significant failure rate, as well as the high stress levels related to deadline extensions, experienced by those writing a thesis.

In pursuit of a long-term teaching vocation, The Thesis Coach was formed as a business for academic performance coaching. It offers, through a unique methodology, individual mentoring, coaching and support for interested, ambitious students. Caroline developed The Dale Method from proven management techniques, several tertiary qualifications in psychology and evidenced-based coaching theory.

Caroline's commitment to improving her methodology to stay abreast of current theories and her natural interest in the science of human behaviour keep her inspired. She is also dedicated to health and wellness, supported by a focus on good nutrition and daily walking.

Caroline holds a BA Hons Psychology (Unisa), BA Psychology (cum laude) (Unisa), PGDip Addiction Care (Stellenbosch), and an MPhil Management Coaching from the University of Stellenbosch Business School.

Caroline can be contacted at:

Email: caroline@thethesiscoach.com| Website: www.thethesiscoach.com LinkedIn business: the-thesis-coach-pty-limited | LinkedIn personal: carolineydale | FaceBook business: TheThesisCoach | YouTube Channel: The Thesis Coach Caroline Dale

FOREWORD

I am a retired stockbroker. During my career, I participated in the development of three reputable, successful stockbroking firms that were members of the Johannesburg Securities Exchange (JSE). Two of these were controlled from abroad. These three firms serviced local and international investors in South African equities.

The first, Ed Hern, Rudolph, operated during the time of the open outcry market, which was in due course replaced by electronic trading.

I met and hired Caroline Dale during 1987 to set up and develop an information technology (IT) function in anticipation of said electronic trading. Caroline set up this function from scratch and systematically developed it into an indispensable part of the firm. She displayed a great ability to create and execute computerised programmes, on time and within budget.

At that time, mining stocks formed the backbone of the JSE. Almost single-handedly, Caroline created a complex set of programmes to continually update the valuation of mining stocks. This enabled Ed Hern, Rudolph to secure second place in the annual financial institutional ratings for gold research. Our investment research into the Industrial and Banking sectors of the JSE was similarly highly rated. As a result, Ed Hern, Rudolph was rated as one of the top three brokers on the JSE.

A feature of the advent of screen trading at the South African equity market was the acquisition of the local stockbroking partnerships by major banking institutions during the 1990s. Ed Hern, Rudolph was sold to NatWest.

Caroline was subsequently offered a senior position at the JSE itself. There she established and developed the IT projects office reporting directly to the JSE EXCO. This new function was vital for the JSE to keep abreast of the rapid changes taking place in international financial markets. Again, her office was a tremendous success.

Caroline left the JSE to shoulder most of the responsibilities for the family as her husband pursued career opportunities outside the RSA. During this time, she acquired several tertiary academic qualifications, the most recent an MPhil in executive coaching from Stellenbosch.

A large proportion of postgraduate students at most educational institutions need thesis extensions at one time or another. I have personal experience of this from my own MBA. Many of those on extensions fail to submit and thus fail their degree.

Given her ordered mind, work ethic, formidable experience, and track record in business, I have no doubt that Caroline, who achieved Cum Laude for her own thesis, can help many postgraduate students to succeed. This book is a blueprint for that success.

Johann Blersch
BCom CA(SA) MBA

PREFACE

As I reflect on my life, the opportunities I've taken or missed, I experience a certain amount of disappointment with my personal and professional development. Some days the voices whispering that I haven't done enough or worked hard enough are insistent.

Then I realise that it takes distance and downtime to reflect and acknowledge progress and measure it in context. Conversations with my family, colleagues and friends help me to gather a degree of perspective when it comes to evaluating my performance. Like all perfectionists, I focus on my perceived failures.

From a different perspective, I must acknowledge how proud I am of much of the progress I have made. My experience as a mature student has transformed my career into vocation and purpose that I could not find in the past. It began with my wanting to become a schoolteacher, then accountant, finding my way in the world of business analysis, information technology, and project management. And finally, with my innate love of books, libraries, university buildings, campus vibes and learning, I have found my niche in the world: a professional academic performance and thesis coach.

My start-up, now entering its fifth year, has passed many milestones and continues to grow. I have every reason to be proud of that. And, I have plenty to look forward to. I have some exciting marketing and expansion ideas which could take my business to a new level after publication of this, my first book.

I love my work. To engage with people who are intent on personal growth and expanding their worlds with postgraduate qualifications is an honour and a great privilege. I have met and coached the most inspiring and tenacious people. It is deeply fulfilling work that I am lucky to have found. The countless moving testimonials from those who I've coached through the maze of thesis writing motivate me to ensure that I continue to help as many people as possible to graduate.

I hope all my readers find time for deep reflection. Be kind to yourself and never forget how far you've come. I hope this book will help you over the finishing line.

ACKNOWLEDGEMENTS

I completed my own MPhil in 2017. Had you told me then I would be publishing a book, I would have thought you a candidate for the asylum.

Writing a book is challenging, requiring patience, knowledge, dedication and time, not only from the author but also those in support roles. In many ways, this task has been a journey of learning and has given me the inspiration to write a better book next time.

I would like to start by thanking my student clients without whom I wouldn't have the experience nor data to write about. I have learnt from you what it takes to overcome the obstacles to submitting a thesis, including ever present stress.

I am grateful to my husband, Tom, who has lovingly and patiently endured my writing this book. He stood by my side offering advice, feedback, editing services, and excellent food and wine. Looking forward to relaxing and unwinding after hours of exhausting thinking and typing made a real difference. Thank you.

To my special girls, Samantha and Angel, who support me unconditionally. Thank you both; your continued belief in me is precious. To my sister, Debs, I know you have my back no matter what the circumstances – I am forever grateful. To my dad, your presence, love and support continues to shine on in all of us, your girls.

To my friend and colleague, Cindi Paige (author), who spent three years writing blogs for my website and kept me focused when the going was tough. To Cherice Torr, who, as a consummate professional graphic designer, produces the most creative infographics and social media marketing visuals. The support I have and continue to receive from you both makes the world of difference to me, thank you.

I am proud that the Stellenbosch University Business School (USB) is my alma mater. Thank you to the faculty and lecturers who taught me and built my self-confidence. Special thanks to Dorrian Aiken, Ruth Albertyn, Roger Maitland and Salome van Coller-Peter. Your experience and knowledge were invaluable.

My USB workgroup, Sarah Arnot, Deborah Williams and Victor Kotze, who pushed me to keep my dream of coaching postgraduate students alive. They continue to support my work and I am grateful for their support, goodwill, constructive feedback and belief in me as a coach. Thank you.

Finally, thank you to my publisher, Wilhelm Crous and his team, who have turned this dream into reality. Your belief in this book from day one stirred the motivation to help me persevere.

INTRODUCTION

Why I wrote this book

There are about 100,000 postgraduate students in South Africa (RSA) and neighbouring countries at any given time. Of these, the majority are probably on extensions to complete their thesis. Such extensions are of finite duration and as a result, a significant number of candidates fail to graduate because they cannot submit a thesis on time. Even though my husband explained this to me after his own MBA, as did my ex-boss at the Johannesburg Securities Exchange (JSE) and several others, I did not connect these dots until I began the MPhil in management coaching at the University of Stellenbosch Business School (USB).

After graduating cum laude for my thesis, a process which precipitated great stress, I generated a personal mission which wove several strands of my life experience to date, together. This mission is to significantly improve the proportion of postgraduate students who submit a good thesis on time and successfully graduate. I intend to disseminate the methodology I have developed (The Dale Method) to enable academic students to overcome the challenges of thesis writing.

My most impressive student was on the brink of failure six weeks before his submission deadline. I coached him intensively using The Dale Method and he duly graduated six weeks later with a cum laude for his thesis.

This book is my current best attempt to spread The Dale Method across as wide an audience as possible in Southern Africa, and indeed in due course, the rest of the world.

I trust you will find it useful and helpful in "getting your life back".

The book has been designed to help students in academia graduate at the highest level of which they are capable. It simultaneously fulfils my dream of becoming a valued and respected coach, mentor and author. I am inspired by facilitating growth. My own academic and coaching journey helped me to identify the challenges we face during the process of growth inherent in writing a successful thesis. I believe that each student who fails to graduate detracts from the economy of the RSA. Conversely, each additional graduate contributes positively!

The process of writing my own master's thesis helped me to refine my thoughts on the contents of this book. It also gave me a framework, which I am sharing with you, within which to discuss the pertinent issues faced by all postgraduate students. The themes and findings that emerged from my research have been an invaluable guide to recording my journey in writing.

Why you must read it

When you begin your postgraduate degree, you commit to submitting a thesis at the required standard before you graduate. Failure to submit a thesis on time results in prolonged periods of misery and serious stress because of years of delay in completing this project.

Submitting a good thesis is difficult but not impossible. Personally, I was unable to find a practical, useful methodology to guide me along my way, so I created my own.

As your academic year begins, the assignments, activities or the thesis itself will cause you to struggle. You will have setbacks and disappointments, but you will experience feelings of achievement and success if you put in the work and seek help when you need it.

The most crucial action you can take right now is to reorient your mindset and get your systems in place. This will be the foundation from which your planning will evolve.

> *"You do not rise to the level of your goals. You fall to the level of your systems. Your goal is your desired outcome. Your system is the collection of daily habits that will get you there. This year, spend less time focusing on outcomes and more time focusing on the habits that precede the results."*

Many times, in my practice as a coach, I've watched students with the appropriate systems and daily habits succeed beyond their own expectations. Many of their peers who push back against planning and working in discrete, incremental sections, struggle to stay afloat from day one.

The task of writing your thesis is the proverbial banquet that you can't consume at a single sitting. No matter how smart you are, I assure you, there is no way to get the best result without breaking the project down into logical, manageable sections. This approach precipitated the synthesis of The Dale Method.

ACCOUNTABILITY **PARTNER**

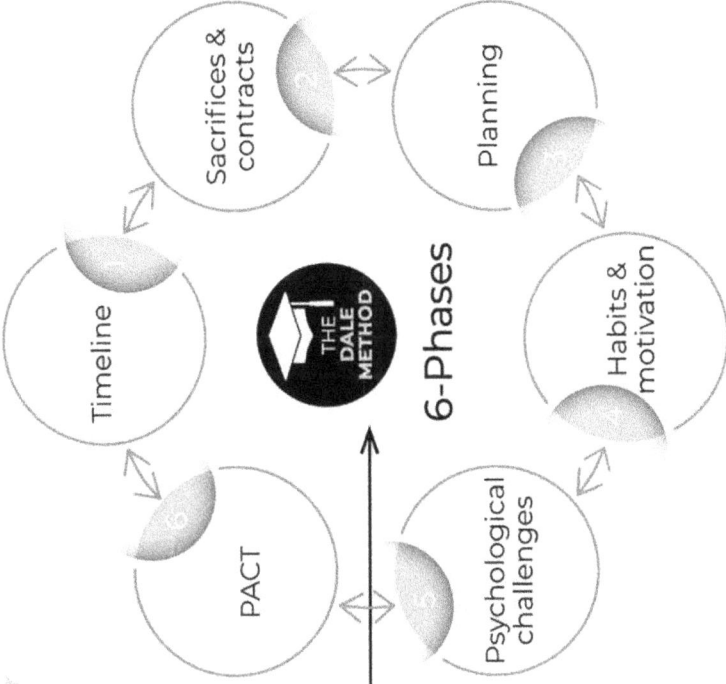

6-Phases

THE DALE METHOD

Values
Drives topic choice
&
Commitment

Sacrifices & contracts

Planning

Habits & motivation

Psychological challenges

PACT

Timeline

The Dale Method is built from a unique blend of evidence-based coaching, psychological theories and personal experience. It is a tried and tested formula for academic success, for any year of study, or for writing your thesis itself.

The 6-phase methodology addresses all the elements of postgraduate study, resulting in the student feeling in control throughout the year: (1) timelines; (2) sacrifices and contracting; (3) habits and motivation; (4) planning; (5) psychological challenges; and (6) PACT. These phases are not linear but cyclical and flexible in nature; the individual moves in and out of each phase depending on the immediate challenge.

It was inappropriate for me to structure the book into a chapter for each of the six phases. These are ever-present throughout your thesis process.

I emphasise that the book is a practical guide which focuses primarily on the overall process and necessary systems for achieving your deadlines. It does not provide help with specific content or how to conduct a sound study: this is the work of the student and their supervisor or any other leading expert in the field of research. I use the term 'supervisor' synonymously with 'advisor' or 'chairperson'.

The difference between success and failure in any endeavour is motivation. Once you divide the overall project into its logical components and complete these, the consequent feelings associated with success will maintain a high level of motivation.

This book is geared to master's and PhD students, but the principles and techniques have been successfully used for those on any other academic quest. For this reason, I trust that the material will be used for years to come as the new crop of students face future challenging projects. For consistency and readability, I use the term 'thesis' interchangeably with 'dissertation' and 'research project'.

I hope this book offers practical guidance and motivation during your thesis journey. My aim is to provide you with confidence and techniques to alleviate misery, stress and anxiety. In addition, I wish you the most rewarding study year: enjoy the process, savour the learning, be authentic, and most importantly, stand up for what you believe in.

CHAPTER 1

SUPERVISOR RELATIONS – CHALLENGES AND SOLUTIONS

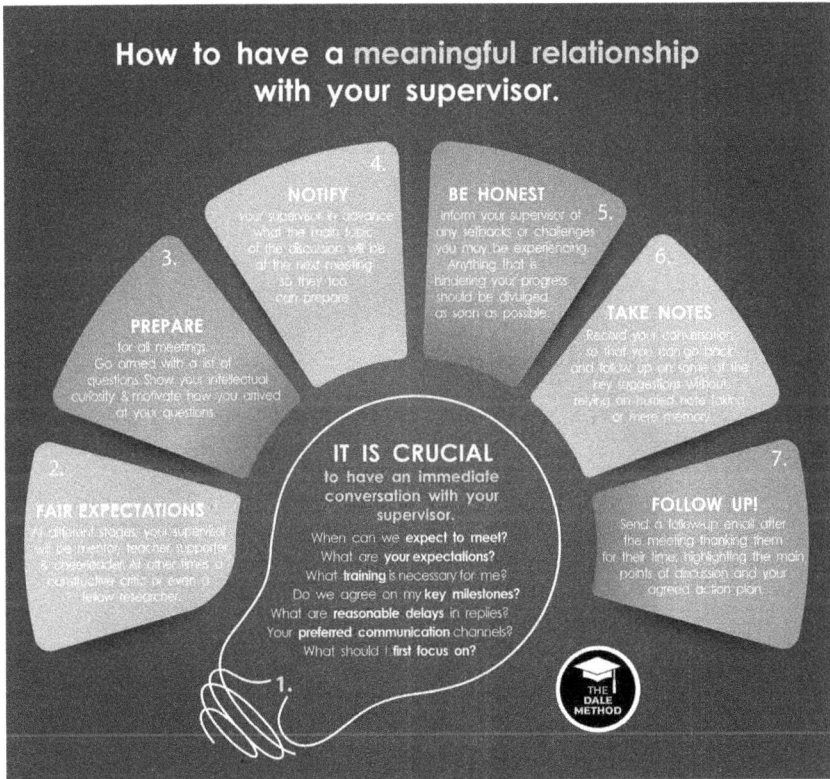

How to have a meaningful relationship with your supervisor.

4.
NOTIFY
your supervisor in advance what the main topic of the discussion will be at the next meeting, so they too can prepare.

BE HONEST
Inform your supervisor of any setbacks or challenges you may be experiencing. Anything that is hindering your progress should be divulged as soon as possible.

5.

6.
TAKE NOTES
Record your conversations so that you can go back and follow up on some of the key suggestions without relying on hurried note taking or mere memory.

3.
PREPARE
for all meetings. Go armed with a list of questions. Show your intellectual curiosity & motivate how you arrived at your questions.

IT IS CRUCIAL
to have an immediate conversation with your supervisor.
When can we **expect to meet?**
What are **your expectations?**
What **training** is necessary for me?
Do we agree on my **key milestones?**
What are **reasonable delays** in replies?
Your **preferred communication** channels?
What should I **first focus on?**

2.
FAIR EXPECTATIONS
At different stages, your supervisor will be mentor, teacher, supporter & cheerleader. At other times a constructive critic or even a fellow researcher.

7.
FOLLOW UP!
Send a follow-up email after the meeting thanking them for their time, highlighting the main points of discussion and your agreed action plan.

1.

THE DALE METHOD

The challenge

One of the biggest challenges students face when writing their thesis is managing an effective relationship with their supervisor. Many of my clients experience feelings of dread at the thought of scheduled supervisor meetings. They often leave the meetings feeling less motivated and overwhelmed, especially if they feel that the supervisor's input or lack thereof has not addressed relevant issues, let alone added value to their work. This frequently causes frustration, anxiety and stress.

By working through these challenges during coaching conversations with my clients, I have gained valuable insights into this serious impasse. The problem is usually a lack of communication between the student and their supervisor.

This is primarily because the student aims for perfection: the perfect topic choice, the perfect research question, the perfect list of aims and objectives, or the perfect literature review (LR). And when these aren't perfect (because they won't be), they withdraw from talking to the one person who can help them. They shy away from interaction because they fear their work is not good enough.

This aiming for perfection results in feelings of doubt, fear and other negative emotional triggers. As a result, they feel helpless and unable to communicate effectively or with confidence.

Your supervisor is vital to the success of your thesis and is there to guide, lead and teach you. Take time to cultivate and nurture a healthy relationship by engaging in regular and honest communication.

I built a fulfilling relationship with my supervisor during my thesis year. We are now friends and coaching colleagues.

The solution

Acknowledge that this relationship is key whilst writing your thesis. Three points provide useful guidance on how to foster and nurture a more meaningful relationship: (1) change your mindset; (2) take charge; and (3) cultivate a mature approach.

Change your mindset

As challenging as it is, take a step back. Shift your perception of the situation by not allowing your feelings to control you when your work is not perfect the first, second or even third time; see it as an opportunity to grow and improve. Never forget that growing and learning is exactly what you signed up for.

Take charge

Although your supervisor is an esteemed academic and deserving of your respect, remember that the successful completion of your thesis is your responsibility alone. This means that you are in charge and must take an active approach when managing this vital relationship.

It is crucial to set aside some time early in the process to have a conversation on how things are likely to work. Your university may provide a ready-made template or checklist for this. If not, the questions below are a good start:

- How often and for how long can we expect to meet?

- What are your preferred communication channels?

- What are reasonable delays in replies to emails or messages?

- Do you agree with my key milestones?

- What are your expectations in terms of delivery dates and content?

- What must I focus on before our next meeting?

- What training is necessary to help me develop as a researcher?

In many ways, this relationship is unlike any other professional or personal one. At specific stages, your supervisor may play different roles: your mentor, teacher, supporter and cheerleader. At other times they become your constructive critic or even a fellow researcher. Your supervisor is only human, just like yourself, and even if you don't 'gel' on a personal level, you may still have a very successful professional relationship. Be realistic with your demands and expectations. Supervisors are busy academics and researchers, often juggling teaching, research, pastoral, administrative and family roles.

Cultivate a mature approach

Prepare. This means being prepared for all meetings. Go armed with a list of questions. Show your intellectual curiosity by discussing your thought processes and motivate how you arrived at your questions. This illustrates dedication, care for your topic and a strong work ethic. You don't want to walk away from a supervisor session not having your questions answered or feeling you could have used your time more constructively. Notify her in advance as to the main topic of the forthcoming discussion with a carefully compiled agenda. This will give her the opportunity to prepare and will ensure that your limited time is used effectively.

Be honest. Inform your supervisor of any setbacks or challenges you may be experiencing, even if they are personal. Anything that is hindering your progress must be divulged as soon as possible. She might not be able to solve your issues, but it will give her insight into why a submission may be late or of lower quality. Showing that you have doubts or concerns or asking for help are not signs of weakness, but a conscious decision to want to succeed.

- Identify where you need training or help.

- Share your concerns about where your project is and where it is going.

- Ask about techniques, resources and recommended reading that could help.

Take notes. Either take written notes or ask if you may record your conversations. It is valuable to go back and follow up on some of the key suggestions without relying on your memory. If you record, you create the opportunity to listen intently after the meeting, without worrying about catching every word or phrase.

Follow up. Send a follow-up email after the meeting thanking them for their time, highlighting the main points of discussion and your agreed action plan.

Practice resilience. You will find this attribute essential for your success. You need to learn to stand back up when you've been knocked down. Don't take things personally. Show up and face your world; never forget you are constantly learning and it's the setbacks and gut punches that provide the learning. No matter how intimidated you feel, remember that there is no such thing as a stupid question. Your supervisor is there to help you, and you must ask for help when you need it. Your success is their success. Just because they may seem 'off' or 'short' with you in email responses doesn't mean they are brushing you off. Don't assume judgement from them, they are probably just busy.

In summary, I cannot stress this foundation for your work enough. Once you have successfully moved from a bumpy to fruitful relationship with your supervisor, keep it intact. Don't let them down with deadlines, unless necessary. Rather take time from work and fulfil your commitments to them. This will stand you in good stead throughout your whole thesis programme.

CHAPTER 2

TOPIC CHOICE – HOW TO CHOOSE

Thesis Topic Choices

THE DALE METHOD

- ✓ My topic aligns to my personal, and professional top values.
- ☐ My topic is compatible with my academic objectives & background.
- ☐ My topic motivates me. I am passionate about it.
- ☐ My topic is feasible with respect to time, resources, and finances.
- ☐ My topic lends itself to realistic collection of data in my field.
- ☐ My topic represents a key learning objective for me.
- ☐ My topic validates the need for further research.
- ☐ My topic is current & will contribute to trends in my field.
- ☐ My topic excites me enough to get me started.

Rationale

There is no question that your choice of topic is fundamental to every aspect of your research project. I wish to share the rationale for my own thesis as an example.

In March 2007, my brother, Colin, died tragically in a motorcycle accident. He was 34 years old. We had both suffered the loss of our mother to a motor car accident when I was six and Colin two. Unfortunately, Colin's life was ripped apart by the loss of our mother and addiction became his lifelong problem. I don't believe he ever recovered from that loss.

At the time of my master's thesis in executive coaching and after accomplishing postgraduate qualifications in psychology and addiction, I realised that I had been on a quest to find life answers: to the questions of loss, addiction and change. In my thesis, I shared my experiences of introspection, emotional and behaviour examination, change and professional growth, whilst emphasising periods of vulnerability, triumphs, challenges and self-awareness.

Based on personal reflections of coaching others and the analysis of my data, the outcomes of my research influenced and helped me identify my personal coaching identity, the core of my coaching practice, and The Thesis Coach business model.

The inner work and insights I accomplished on this journey improved my understanding of the processes of individual change and corroborated how it features as an essential component of coaching practice.

My topic was aligned with my academic and personal interests. My history and experience provided authenticity and hence created the necessary motivation to keep going. The learning that happened for me gave birth to a new vocation and a genuine coaching identity.

My thesis journey, with all its triumphs, anxieties and fears, will live on as a personal experience and a process of professional and personal development. I trust you will enjoy the motivation to do your own authentic and meaningful research.

How do you choose?

Choosing a relevant thesis topic is critical to success.

What is a thesis topic?

By definition, a thesis is a report submitted to faculty in support of candidature for an academic degree. The report presents the author's topic, research, findings and interpretation. Not all studies have hypotheses, for example when a study is designed to be exploratory (inductive research), there is no formal hypothesis.

You must first think about a problem or phenomenon in your field of interest or expertise. Ultimately, a topic evolves from a problem that you see every day.

Aim for relevant instead of ground-breaking research

Many students start out with lofty ideals of writing a ground-breaking paper that will be recognised and published in an academic journal. The clock ticks, and too much time is spent thinking up "the next best thing" simply for the sake of being "the next best thing". This can be debilitating. Focus on solving a real and meaningful problem for which solid theoretical literature and empirical results are available and accessible.

What, in your field of interest, is a problem that keeps you awake at night, inspires you, or keeps your interest piqued?

How to get started

Start by choosing a broad area of study within your field. Based on questions you know exist in this area, narrow the field down to a niche that is a specific problem to be solved, which is of clear interest to you.

Begin by brainstorming and free-writing to get your mind moving in the right direction. Talk to others about your ideas and research these topics to determine the availability and accessibility of information and data. Then create a shortlist of potential options and, if you already have one, test them with your supervisor or possibly some other faculty sponsor.

Test the viability of your thesis topic choice

A simple but effective exercise is to list all your ideas for a thesis topic. Don't hold back. Think hard. Then rate each of the topics on a scale of 1-10 using the criteria listed below. The topic that scores highest in one or more of the criteria below, should be investigated as the best option.

- My topic aligns with my academic and personal interests.
- My topic is compatible with my academic objectives and background.
- My topic motivates and inspires me.
- My topic is feasible with respect to time, resources, and finances.
- My topic lends itself to a realistic collection of data in my field.
- My topic represents a key learning objective for me.
- My topic validates the need for further research.
- My topic is current and will contribute to trends in my field.
- My topic excites me enough to get me started.

Once you've chosen your topic, create a habit and become interactive with it every day. You must develop an intimate relationship with your topic to stay engaged and committed. Expect to feel frustrated at times but never forget that it's okay to take a short break and practice some self-reflection and/or self-compassion. The key is simple: never give up and aim to make progress, albeit small, every day.

Here's my professional advice on how to succeed

Don't wait for inspiration, just get started. Topic choices will not just appear magically. You will find thoughts being generated as you delve deeper into the research in your field. When you work in a methodical fashion, thoughts will form into new ideas as you familiarise yourself with what is out there and what you want to do.

Turn your inspiration into a daily habit. Inspiration alone won't keep you going, you must develop that habit.

The problem drives the process. Do not jump into your investigation before you understand and define your research problem and the thesis statement. This is the foundation for your research and drives the whole process.

Don't panic, your title will evolve. It is not necessary to finalise your title at the beginning. Let it evolve as you dig deeper into the research out there. Your own personal and academic objectives will gain clarity and highlight themselves during your preliminary research actions. You will have "aha" moments during this time; let them flourish. And challenge your peers to be thinking partners to help develop and clarify your thoughts.

Avoid perfectionism like the plague. You will not find the "perfect" topic for yourself in your field. Perfectionism is a form of procrastination and at any stage of your thesis journey is an enemy. Avoid it from the start.

Simplicity is key. We all want to change the world. At some stage, you may consider a research project that feels big and bold: remember, these amazing, beautiful, and altruistic ideals can set you up for failure.

Don't read too much. Continual reading may become an excuse for procrastination, which is another thesis journey enemy. A review of available sources will suffice to reveal your thesis topic. This is not a LR. Scan read your sources to get a general overview of what other academics have studied, researched, and written.

Ask for help. Your supervisor, peers, faculty members and coach will accelerate your process.

Do you want a distinction? Ask your supervisor how and include her feedback in your strategy.

In summary, topic choice is crucial to your thesis success. You cannot build a superstructure on a weak foundation. Understand that your traits and experiences will influence your progress and what you bring to your research will make it authentic.

CHAPTER 3

THESIS FRAMEWORK – THE 5 CHAPTERS

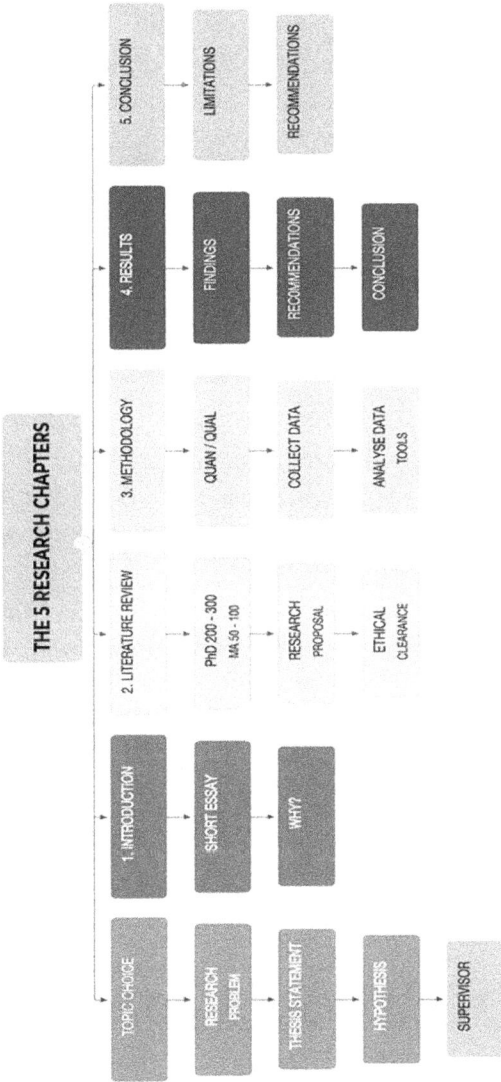

THE 5 RESEARCH CHAPTERS

1. INTRODUCTION
- SHORT ESSAY
- WHY?
  - TOPIC CHOICE
  - RESEARCH PROBLEM
  - THESIS STATEMENT
  - HYPOTHESIS
  - SUPERVISOR

2. LITERATURE REVIEW
- PHD 200 - 300 / MA 50 - 100
- RESEARCH PROPOSAL
- ETHICAL CLEARANCE

3. METHODOLOGY
- QUAN / QUAL
- COLLECT DATA
- ANALYSE DATA / TOOLS

4. RESULTS
- FINDINGS
- RECOMMENDATIONS
- CONCLUSION

5. CONCLUSION
- LIMITATIONS
- RECOMMENDATIONS

Most students are quite overwhelmed at the idea that they are tasked to write 80 or more pages for the thesis component of their course, and many do not know where to start. What should the chapter outlines be? What kind of content should be in these chapters?

> *Please download and print your Research Process from my website.*
> *https://www.thethesiscoach.com*

This chapter is intended to provide you with a simple, yet practical, roadmap to getting your thesis document started. The bullet points below serve as a guideline and give you a solid start, but bear in mind that there is a lot more to it than that.

It is imperative that right from the beginning you understand your institution's technical requirements for the actual thesis document: title page layout, margins, font, line spacing, tables and figures descriptions, format of front page, format of table of contents and any other technical aspects that you need to know.

Spend the time you need to get your thesis document set up in your software of choice, in the correct format, and back it up. Get this document onto your desktop, where you see it every day. Now you have a live working document, and you can start populating it with your own work.

Each chapter in your research report should have a brief introduction and summary/conclusion. Your introduction will remind the readers of your research aims and objectives, and provide a roadmap for the chapter so they know what to expect. Wrap up each chapter with a summary. Be concise – a maximum of two paragraphs – and do not add any new information.

With university-specific differences, your thesis will follow this basic format.

THE BEGINNING	
Title page	Crafted to perfection.
Declaration	The work is your own.
Acknowledgements	Give thanks.
Abstract	<ul><li>The abstract is a tight, concise summary.</li><li>It will be the first substantive description of your work read by an external examiner.</li><li>It must represent all the elements of your work in a highly condensed manner.</li><li>It is not an introduction.</li></ul>
List of tables, figures, acronyms	Each on their own page.
THE MIDDLE	
Chapter 1: Introduction	<ul><li>Describes the background for your chosen topic.</li><li>Highlights your research topic and question and describes your aims, objectives, and research questions.</li><li>Describes the purpose and benefits of the study.</li></ul>
Chapter 2: Literature review (LR)	<ul><li>Confirms your keywords/constructs – these determine your search criteria.</li><li>Create an efficient article storage system for easy source access later.</li><li>Organise your references efficiently.</li><li>Understand your reading saturation point.</li></ul>
Chapter 3: Research methodology	<ul><li>Describe the background and design.</li><li>Discuss the explicit data collection and data analysis process you used.</li><li>Explain your data analysis software, if any.</li><li>Discuss your ethical procedures.</li><li>Confirm your methodological fit with your supervisor.</li></ul>

Chapter 4: Results and discussion	• Highlight your findings. • Interpretation of your data. • Contributions and limitations. • Recommendations for further research.
Chapter 5: Conclusion	• Connect all the dots.
THE END	
Reference List	APA, Harvard, university protocol.
Appendices	As referred to in the text.

Chapter 1: Introduction

Start by building an outline of your introduction, which should include three sections: (1) the importance of the research and why you have chosen it; (2) a summary of the existing literature; and (3) your carefully constructed research question or hypothesis. Your intention is to create a compelling story that leads to your research question.

It is essential that your first paragraph provides a powerful introduction about the importance of your topic. It must be something bigger and more important than your research and set the tone to get the reader excited: your audience must be compelled to continue reading. You want to prove that your topic is strong and highlight why. An example:

> *Anxiety is a universal problem which impairs peoples' physical, mental, and cognitive well-being (cite reference). According to research conducted by X (cite reference), anxiety affects more than 22% of adult South Africans who experience at least one panic attack annually. In addition, further studies suggest that approximately 45% of anxiety symptoms can lead to depressive episodes that play a role in suicide attempts (cite reference).*

Your first sentence showcases the overall topic, while the subsequent sentences explain why the topic is strong. Remember to use phrases such as, "It is widely assumed that X", "There is a consensus that X is a prolific problem worldwide".[2]

```
READ

They Say, I Say: The moves that matter in
            academic writing

    Gerald Graff and Cathy Birkenstein
```

In the paragraphs that cover section two, provide an overview of the relevant scientific literature. What is already known? Where are the gaps and what questions remain open? Are there conflicts in the literature? Use phrases such as, "Several studies have shown that...", "While some studies suggested X, others suggested Y", "The contrast between them proposes X".[3]

In the paragraphs that cover section three, state your research question or hypothesis. Summarise a rough explanation of your research stating what you tested or explored, how many research participants you used, and your underlying methodology.

Writing hooks

A vital component of effective thesis writing is to captivate your audience from the start; they must be compelled to read more. Finding the right hook is pivotal to achieving this objective. A hook is the first couple of sentences in the introduction of your report which is designed specifically to captivate your audience.

It is difficult to craft that hook; with the vast amount of content passing through people's lives daily, you are competing for your reader's attention. People are easily distracted, so if you don't hook them straight away, you will lose them. Remember, your hook must be congruent and relevant to your topic.

This is an exciting avenue of writing to explore and will stand you in good stead throughout your thesis and any further writing projects. Here are the five most common ones.

Ask an open-ended question. This immediately captures attention and leaves the reader thinking, wanting to explore, and wanting an answer. Not just a yes or no answer, something to ponder.

Quote an impressive statistic related to your field. This fact latches your audience afnd keeps them motivated to learn more right from the beginning. It gives them confidence in your research and expertise and builds trust.

Choose a compelling and relevant quotation. These words will provide rich meaning and credibility and grab immediate attention. They must 100% align with your work and be comprehensively explained so as not to confuse your reader.

Make a bold and solid statement. Even if the reader is ambivalent about your statement, they will be naturally curious and intrigued to watch you assert your position.

Use an anecdotal hook if doing a narrative essay. This is a powerful way to grab attention because it's intimate and possibly vulnerable. This sharing can open the heart of your reader and compel them to keep reading out of care.

Chapter 2: Literature review

The second chapter of your thesis is the LR, and it is this segment of the written work that often presents as a major stumbling block for students. The biggest issue is not being certain where to start.

What is a literature review?

A LR is the culmination of all your research, succinctly presented and scrutinised for its worth. All that reading and gathering of articles, academic papers, and books you read will feature here. In this chapter, you provide an overview of key findings, concepts, and developments in relation to your research problem or question.

Key elements of an LR

A decent LR does not just summarise sources, it aims to:

- analyse, interpret and critically evaluate the literature;
- demonstrate a thoughtful synthesis of the material and your key constructs by highlighting patterns, themes, conflicts and gaps; and

- show the state of current knowledge in relation to a central research question or hypothesis.

How do you go about it?

Determine your sources. Firstly, refer to your network – anyone you believe has knowledge about your topic or field of research, including your supervisor, faculty, friends, colleagues and authors. Do not be afraid; receive advice from wherever it comes. You will find help where you least expect it, so listen, think and consider all the advice. Secondly, do internet searches and use Google Scholar. Thirdly, identify experts in the field: (1) visit their websites and find overviews of their publications; (2) review their blogs; and (3) check their references for further leads to sources. Finally, check the references on all the relevant sources you find.

Find them. Go to the library and ask the librarian for help. Librarians are accessible and often extremely helpful, but are generally an underutilised resource because students do not always reach out for their help. They will assist with keyword searches, referencing and accessing academic journals. Use Google Scholar to find articles or studies and check the websites of the first authors: consider emailing the first author.

Scan your articles. If the title interests you, this is a worthy start. Read the abstract to determine whether the article is relevant to your topic. If yes, read the introduction to validate relevance and move on to scanning the rest of the document, slowing to read the summary and conclusion.

As you work your way through your sources, begin the writing process – take notes that you can later incorporate into the text of your LR. It is important to keep track of your sources with citations to avoid plagiarism. A technique worth considering is to number each of your articles in one folder. This way you always know exactly how many sources you have and it makes finding articles simple.

Another useful technique is to copy and paste pieces of articles with either precise references or your own reference system (A1, p17) into your LR document. This means that you write while you read, because as you find worthwhile and relevant quotes or explanations they are immediately placed into your written work. Paraphrasing and rearranging this text happens later; the important thing here is to start populating your research report.

Another useful tip is to sort your research into a table that collates important data: date, peer-reviewed, title, keywords, methodology, key findings, limitations and any other information you deem important. This will help you to scrutinise your articles for specific data, it will specify a framework in which to work, and it will provide a summarised view of all your reading.

In summary

1. Search for your sources:

    - Use your constructs/keywords and combinations of them.

    - Use Google Scholar.

    - Contact your university library and find a librarian to help you search.

    - Create only one source folder for literature.

    - Number each of your sources, starting from 1.

2. Create your working document.

    - Ensure you use the correct format – use the right template.

    - Build your table of contents – this is your foundation.

    - Use your constructs/keywords as subcategories in your table of contents for now.

    - You will find as you immerse yourself in the literature and start reading, other themes will arise.

3. Immerse yourself in the literature.

    - Does this source work for you? Find out by skimming each of your articles – do it one by one.

    - Read the abstract – does it resonate with your topic?

    - Read the conclusion – does it make sense to you?

- Scan read the methodology – is this what you are thinking?
- Scan read the rest of the document.
- Categorise (colour code) your document – good, medium, bad.
- Your research question will start to break itself down into sub-sections.

4. Start reading and populating chapter 2 in your research report.

- Start reading from article number 1.
- Choose the articles you categorised as good first.
- Anything you read that feels important to you, copy and paste into chapter 2 in the sub section you have already formulated.
- This would be plagiarism, so reference it (A1, p̄3 = article 1, page 3). You can paraphrase this later – just get the words into the right sections.

5. Analyse and synthesise for your readers.

- What are the common themes developing from your sources?
- Are they reporting similar or different things?
- Where do these themes feature in the subcategories of your topic and research question?
- Is there a history of the topic that evolves (looking at the source in chronological order)?

> It is never too early to start writing.
> It is always easier to edit than to write the first draft.

Mind over matter

The LR is a vital and substantial part of your paper, so getting this part done means overcoming a major hurdle. But it's not easy. Naturally, we all feel resistance to tackling work that we deem complicated and hard to do. Many students lean towards procrastination by putting off the big task while tackling other less important tasks because this still makes them feel productive. Or maybe you've suddenly had an overwhelming urge to reorganise the kitchen cupboards? Unfortunately, that's still procrastination and you'll have to overcome the resistance to avoid getting started.

Strategies to overcome resistance

Recognise that you're in resistance mode. This is the first step – identify your state of mind, acknowledge what it is, and own it. Walk away from the situation and question yourself. Uncover that which is standing in your way and find a way to manage it.

Start with a clean slate. Do not feel frustrated with yourself over the tasks you didn't complete yesterday. Do not let one unproductive day run into many. This is a new day, start again.

Do at least one small thing. Resistance is most powerful when it makes you feel incredibly overwhelmed by all you must do, because the more overwhelmed you are, the more likely you are to embrace the "there's too much to do so I'll do nothing" attitude. Feeling too overwhelmed can be paralysing and it's another trick resistance uses to keep you in a state of unproductivity. Combat the feeling of being overwhelmed by doing just one small, achievable thing, for example, today I'm going to write 100 words for my thesis. Usually committing and achieving just a small goal is enough to get you unstuck and moving forward.

Try a new location or tactic. Switch things around to combat resistance because it throws things off. If you have a routine that isn't working, try something new, such as moving your workspace to a new location.

Be open to success. If you embrace resistance daily, you begin to identify with it; it becomes a part of who you are and of your routine, which diminishes your chance of success. Change your mindset and visualise the finish line – your graduation date.

Ask for help. Working with a mentor, coach, colleague, faculty member or friend will help you, as far as possible, with blocks you must overcome. They will provide practical strategies and support throughout your studies.

Remember, resistance is normal, especially when facing a complex task like writing a LR, but you must put mind over matter and get the job done.

Test your LR against these questions

- Is the purpose (aims and objectives) of your research clear and concise?

- Is your rationale (explanation of the fundamental reasons) clear and concise?

- Are your cited sources credible (known for their work on the topic)?

- Is the rationale for your chosen methodology articulate?

- Is your methodology justifiable given your research objectives?

- Is your LR clearly written and easy to understand?

Chapter 3: Methodology – the research process

Your methodology chapter is where you comprehensively inform readers of your research design choices and justify your reasons. This chapter is important because it exhibits your understanding of academic research design theory, illustrates that your findings will be credible, and provides a framework for your research to be replicated (it is important for academic research to build on what has been done previously and compare the results).

Another significant aspect of the methodology chapter is that it provides the opportunity for you to establish and highlight any limitations (methodological problems) you may have found. Your ability to illustrate how you mitigated these challenges and how your study is still worthwhile despite these shortcomings will contribute towards your marks.

This chapter is exciting but complex because you will be writing it, as part of your research proposal, before you conduct your research. As you refine your thinking, your intended methodology (as per your proposal) may change. In other words, your initial writing will be written in the future tense, and after the research is conducted, the chapter will be written in past tense.

Writing up the methodology chapter

Once again, ensure you are familiar with the exact format and contents prescribed, as this varies depending on the university and field of study.

Locate a few full studies (not articles) submitted in your field (e.g., social sciences, finance, psychology, technology) with a similar topic idea and review them. Find a generic structure for the methodology chapter typically applied to this field.

I recommend that you save the methodology chapter format to your desktop and start by creating a table of contents. This will be non-specific for now, but you can embellish or refine it as you proceed. This gives you direction and helps guide your thinking; it will be your framework. This is the case for every chapter of your research report, because if you don't know where you are headed, your narrative and flow will suffer.

Remember, if you can't articulate – either verbally or in writing – exactly how you intend to conduct this research, you will not be able to action it. Close your eyes and write or type each step of the process.

Research design

Research philosophy. Present your research philosophy (underlying beliefs or world view) about how your data were collected and analysed. Two common philosophies are **positivism** (usually quantitative/objective) and **interpretivism** (usually qualitative/subjective), but there are more. Before you finalise your design, investigate all of them and find out which one best aligns with your topic and suits the field. This decision must be validated with your supervisor, who will help you articulate and outline it clearly with justification. Spend time on this part of the project because it is the core of your research and will determine how you make other key design choices.

Research type. Firstly, describe whether your research was **inductive** (usually exploratory, where theory is generated from the collected data) or **deductive** (usually confirms existing theory and builds onto it). Secondly, related to this decision is your choice of **quantitative** (quantity with statistics), **qualitative** (quality with meaning), or **mixed methods** (a bit of both) research. Remember, this must align with your philosophy choice and be justified.

Research strategy. In other words, your action plan. You must stipulate, precisely, how this study was conducted based on your aims. Again, there are several research strategies, e.g., ethnography, autoethnography, action research, experiments, phenomenology. Schedule time to fully appreciate this variety on offer and confirm your selection with your supervisor. The availability of time and other practical constraints will determine whether you choose a **cross-sectional** or a **longitudinal** data collection method.

Data collection. Firstly, how did you find your sample: (1) **probability** (random/representative) or (2) **non-probability** (non-random/non-representative) sampling? Secondly, how did you collect your data: (1) a survey (usually quantitative) or (2) interviews/focus groups (usually qualitative)? This section must be explicit. Do not believe that any small detail is insignificant. Your reader must be clear on exactly what you did.

Data analysis. Justify and be specific about the methods or techniques you used. Before you write this chapter, imagine you have all these data in your hands, and they're all over the place. What are you going to do with them? The main consideration is whether you outsource, learn to do it digitally, or do it manually. There are a variety of different opinions so ultimately this will be your choice. Find out what others have done, get advice from peers, or discuss with faculty – just be comfortable with your selection.

Your choice will depend on the core of your design, and you will become familiar with these constructs: (1) thematic, discourse and content analysis (usually qualitative); or (2) description or inferential statistics (usually quantitative).

Conclude with a brief summary of the chapter.

Chapter 4: Results and discussion

This chapter is one of the most important in your research report because it informs the reader of what you have found in terms of the data you collected. At this stage, you will have completed your data analysis, and will start the reporting work. This chapter is typically called 'Results', but may also be called the 'Analysis and findings' chapter.

You will be reporting on the results of either a quantitative or qualitative data analysis. These are obviously different so you must confirm the correct protocol for reporting. You will present your data using a concise text narrative, supported by graphs and tables. This will provide the reader with a valuable, visually appealing account of your findings and will highlight any unusual findings you may have encountered.

Sometimes the university requires that you present your findings and discussion in chapter 4, or they stipulate that the discussion occurs in the next chapter, so you'll need to find this out. It is important that you recognise that presenting your findings is different to interpreting these findings. In other words, the results describe your collected data (quantitative or qualitative), while the discussion is your interpretation of the data. This requires that you link your findings to prior research (your LR) and of course, link back to your research aims, objectives or questions.

What to include. In my experience, most students end their analysis with vast amounts of data, not all of which are necessary to include in this write-up; cut through the noise and focus. Decide what is most relevant, what resonates most with your topic, what aligns most with the purpose of your study and what feels interesting and fresh.

Do not feel you have wasted time with the analysis; having heaps of data proves that you have engaged with, and have a deep understanding of, the dataset. Relevance is vital so constantly refer to your aims, objectives and questions to remain aligned.

Brief introduction to the chapter. As with all chapters of your thesis, you must begin this chapter with an overview of what happens in the chapter and why. This is where you revisit your research purpose, aims, objectives and questions, as these are the driving force behind your entire research project and of course inform this chapter. In this introduction, you may enlighten your readers about the representativeness of your sample by exhibiting demographic information, before explaining your plan for the interpretation.

This section must be short (maximum of two paragraphs), concise and informative. It is imperative that you weave a golden thread throughout the entire research report. This is done by re-iterating the research questions into this section to ensure flow.

Outline the structure for this chapter. Ask yourself what statistical analysis (quantitative) or thematic analysis (qualitative) specifically helps you to address your research questions and draw a rough outline of your findings. Think about the key points that you have encountered and want to raise as answers to these questions as part of your discussion. Create chapter subsections to address, in order of importance, the specific tests or transcripts you feel best address your questions.

Sample demographic data. You will define an overview of the demographics of your sample (participants or respondents): (1) age range; (2) ethnicity distribution; (3) living location; (4) gender distribution; (5) and other. This helps with generalising or contextualising your findings when you are interpreting your data. This will also be dependent on your research design, so ask for your supervisor's guidance on this one. This demographic may be a significant factor when interpreting your data, so it's important to understand and present it clearly.

Present the analysed data. This will be different for quantitative (presents statistics) and qualitative data (presents themes). The text narrative must be comprehensible for the reader; repetition and overlap will be utterly confusing. Remember they are reading this for the first and not 100th time.

Chapter summary. As with the chapter introduction, this must be short and sweet, but succinct. Provide a brief write-up of the key findings most relevant to your research objectives and questions, and include a chapter flow into either the discussion or conclusion.

Note:

- All tables, graphs or diagrams that categorise your data in themes or variables are an effective way to present your data. Colour coding adds to the visual appeal and makes the information more digestible and easier to read.

- Label your figures clearly – do not miss the vertical and horizontal axis titles.

- The text write-up must not rely on the figures and tables; these must be purely complementary.

- All findings are to be reported in the past tense.

- The chapter must be logically and sequentially structured.

- Use the help of a graphic designer to draw your graphs and tables.

- Tweak this chapter – it is important. Read and read again. You must provide enough information to answer your research questions and avoid using superfluous data.

- Do not make assumptions that the reader has experience in your field. You do not want to confuse them.

- Review other thesis reports from your university, especially the findings and discussion chapters. Become familiar with the requirements.

It is important to acknowledge the limitations of your study. Limitations can be found in any part of your study (scope, theory, analysis method, sample, collection, etc.). Your study will not be diminished by acknowledging these limitations. Rather, owning them is a true indicator of high-quality research and is considered a strength, not a weakness. You are welcome to remind the reader of the value of your topic and how the limitations can be used for further, improved research.

Recommendations for application and suggestions for future research. Provide recommendations for implementing the findings of your work (application), and suggestions for further research in the future.

Chapter 5: Conclusion

The finish line is in sight, and it is time to conclude. In my experience, this is sometimes the worst part of essay writing. Trying to condense your entire study into a concise, articulate and compelling conclusion that emphasises the significance of your work is easier said than done. Spend time and ruminate on how to get this right.

Formulate a strategy. You want to leave your readers with an end that adds texture and colour to your discussion. Contemplate the broader matters and implications of your research and perhaps connect all the dots to your findings. It is your personal choice if you want to find someone to help you brainstorm this final chapter. Ultimately, it is imperative that your reader perceives that you have accomplished what you set out to do.

Write a worthy conclusion. Start by paraphrasing your topic and purpose to remind your reader, giving a fresh perspective. Gather your supporting points and connect the dots in a way that illustrates the importance of the arguments. This is an intuitive process, so feel your work, think deeply about what you've accomplished, and do not just summarise. Your intention is to leave the reader with thought-provoking ideas and a sense of hope for your work and any further opportunities for research.

Ask yourself, "So what?" All research lecturers ask this question. It is standard protocol when doing any academic writing (even in school days, this was a question asked by teachers). These questions reign: "So what?", "Why does it matter?", "Who cares?" Ask this of yourself throughout your writing process. Remember that the flow of your research purpose is the golden thread that holds it all together. The conclusion will follow naturally.

Add perspective and a compelling ending. The conclusion is the perfect space for citing a liberating or inspiring quote that speaks directly to your purpose and aligns to your research objectives and questions. Use one of your primary references, an expert in the field, to add some final thoughts. Your closing sentence must be the clincher. You want your reader to feel a sense of enjoyment; that he didn't waste his time; that he learnt something meaningful; and that he got a sense of closure.

Simple thesis report tweaks and tips when crafting a powerful **conclusion** chapter:

- Always confirm your university's structural and formatting preferences for what you need to cover in the conclusion – check this properly.

- Be concise and clear in your thoughts and writing.

- Explicitly answer the research question(s) and address the research aims:

    o Avoid making "bold" claims using words like, "This study proves or disproves X".

    o Be humble but confident in your claims.

- Your conclusion must be more general and high level than your discussion chapter.

    o Do not copy and paste from your discussion chapter, which has a different function and is more intricate.

- The idea is to integrate the key findings in your study. This is not just a summary; it must convey a sense of closure – of pulling it all together based on the larger meaning of the topic. Create a table or diagram to illustrate this integration of findings – ensure this is professionally done.

- Don't include any new findings in your conclusion chapter. These must be presented in the discussion chapter first.

- Your reader must be able to pick up the general purpose and key findings of your research by reading only the introduction and conclusion chapters. These chapters must offer a smooth flow and create their own story. Ask somebody to read yours and give feedback.

- Keep the concluding summary succinct. Possibly use a compelling quote from a referenced source to frame your final thoughts in a different light.

- Consider your closing sentence and end on a positive note, so your audience is pleased they read your paper and learnt something worthwhile.

Research proposal and ethical clearance

Research proposal

A research proposal is prescribed by your university. It is a structured, formal document that clarifies your thinking: **what** you intend to research (your topic), **why** this research is worthwhile (your rationalisation), and **how** you propose to do it (the process).

What you intend to research. Your topic must be clearly articulated in your proposal; be explicit and unambiguous. You will spend time with your supervisor doing this work. It may be time consuming and often frustrating, but this time will be well spent and result in a crystal-clear topic.

Why your research is worthwhile. Simply proposing a topic is not good enough; it must be justified, unique and fill a gap. Refine your thinking, research question/s and the value your research offers with your supervisor.

How you propose to conduct your research. This is important because no matter how impressive and convincing your research topic, if collecting data proves insurmountable or very difficult, it will not be practical or realistic. It is not expected, at the proposal stage, to have a concrete research strategy. It suffices that you have a high-level view of your methodology and you've made some key decisions: (1) qualitative/quantitative approach; (2) collection of data choices (interviews/surveys); and (3) statistical/qualitative analysis (digital or manual).

The length of your research proposal. Please check this with your university because it varies and is dependent on specific requirements such as your field of study (social, science, etc.) and your specific degree. It consists of a combination of your introduction, initial LR and proposed methodology, in other words, the diluted versions of chapters one, two and three. Be certain to check the requirements before you start writing.

Your proposal timeline. A timeline is usually an important part of a thesis project proposal, which offers the reader a broad overview of deliverables and dates, be it days, weeks, months or years. The timeline is a visual representation of your full schedule, including begin and end dates. It is presented chronologically using a visual, colourful map or a linear list. This approach depends on your preferences and other factors such as your workspace and lifestyle.

It makes sense to work your way backwards from the end date. Consider editing, proofreading, feedback from supervisor, reference list checks, creation of graphics or visuals, or that which you envisage taking time. Invest time into this exercise: ask colleagues or peers, ask those who have written a thesis before, and ask Google Scholar.

In summary, the purpose of this proposal is to craft a convincing narrative. It aims to compel the powers that be (faculty, supervisor, university) that your project is research worthy (for your specific degree) and manageable (timeline, resources).

Ethical clearance

Ethical clearance approval is a compulsory and essential step in your research process. The main reason for this is to ensure that you intend to conduct your research in a responsible and ethical way, i.e., there is minimal risk of harming humans (and animals). Ultimately, this approval contends that your research findings will lead to meaningful and beneficial outcomes.

The ethical principles to be considered are standard and universal, but will be relevant to your study: voluntary participation, informed consent, confidentiality, anonymity, do no harm, communication of results, any others relevant.

Ethical clearance will be granted on the basis that any unanticipated issues, changes to your research strategy or plan, or perceived/real harm (physical, social, psychological, financial, other) are reported directly to the university ethics committee.

It is prudent to communicate with your research co-ordinator/s early in your thesis programme, as they will provide you with an ethical clearance checklist and inform you of the process and deadlines. The process is often laborious and requires learning, so schedule time for this task.

Locate the checklist before writing your research proposal, it will prepare you for your ethical application.

It is ethically illegal to begin communicating with potential participants or collecting data before ethical clearance approval. Build this into your timeline and planning. This often creeps up and puts your research programme on hold, which is debilitating, frustrating and will sabotage your plans. See to it that you get this process under control early on.

CHAPTER 4

PROJECT MANAGEMENT

PROJECT MANAGE YOURSELF
TO THE THESIS FINISH LINE

THE DALE METHOD

PHASE 01

Focus on **the title of your research project**, identifying specific goals & objectives. Research the literature & concentrate on your unique topic & research questions with their associated objectives. This phase requires direct communication with your supervisor for input, feedback, & guidance.

PHASE 02

The power of planning & creating timelines. Be realistic & explicit. Identify & build your support team. Be flexible in your planning, acknowledge psychological barriers, potential project killers, & that you are human.

PHASE 03

You physically do the work. This equates to collecting data, analysing data, & extrapolating your findings. It gives you the opportunity to be creative, dig deep to find the answers to your research question/s. This is where you create your masterpiece.

PHASE 04

Taking stock. How are you performing? Presumably you have identified ways in which to measure your own performance. This is an essential part of any project because it addresses accountability and control. Engage with others for feedback: peers, supervisor/s, coach or friends.

PHASE 05

You tie up all the loose ends. You tweak the product. In thesis terms this means articulating your conclusion, summing up the limitations of your study, identifying suggestions for future research, acknowledging those who supported your process.

It is time to take the reins and become your own project manager. You have a limited amount of time and energy in any single day or week; direct them towards your own, personal value-driven and prioritised goals.

The Project Management Institute process

The Project Management Institute (PMI) has described five phases for any project management process: (1) conception and initiation; (2) planning; (3) execution; (4) performance/monitoring; and (5) project closure. I am using this framework in terms of your research project and pointing out how these five phases relate directly to specific phases in thesis writing.

During phase 1, focus on the title of your research project and spend time identifying specific goals and objectives. This part of your thesis project is tiresome and mind-blowing because you tend to wander around in circles trying to find the right wording, and to articulate your thinking on paper feels messy and incoherent. You are then required to research the literature and concentrate on your unique topic and research questions with their associated aims and objectives. This phase requires direct communication with your supervisor and possibly other faculty members for input, feedback and guidance.

Do not underestimate phase 2 – the power of planning and creating timelines. Your focus is to be realistic and explicit in your endeavours. Spend time identifying and building your support team and prepare them for the process ahead. Be flexible in your planning, acknowledge psychological challenges, potential project killers, and that you are human and life happens. At some stage, you may have to reprioritise, get a grip and get back in the game.

During phase 3 you get active and physically do the work. In the thesis process, this equates to collecting data, analysing data and extrapolating your findings. This is the fun part of your research project because it gives you the opportunity to be creative and dig deep to find the answers to your research question/s. This is where you play with your canvas and create your masterpiece. Be flexible with your actionable items and update them daily because they will keep changing.

Phase 4 requires taking stock. How are you performing with respect to your goals and objectives? Presumably you have identified ways in which to measure your own performance. This is an essential part of any project because it addresses accountability and control. Throughout this process, engage with others for feedback: peers, colleagues, supervisor/s, faculty members, mentors, a coach or friends.

During phase 5, you tie up all the loose ends; you tweak the product. In thesis terms, this means articulating your conclusion, summing up the limitations of your study, identifying suggestions for future research, acknowledging those who supported your process (in writing), ensuring your references are perfect, having your work edited, checking that you have adhered to all the technical specifications, and probably numerous other items.

The importance of a timeline

A timeline or multiple timelines are essential to your thesis project: they help organise the work to be done in a chronological sequence; they hold everyone involved accountable for completing the work; and they are known to be effective. For your thesis, I recommend you generate an electronic or paper year planner and dedicate it to your thesis work.

It makes sense to work your way backwards from the end date. Consider the time required for editing, proofreading, incorporating feedback from your supervisor, conducting reference list checks, physically collecting your data, transcribing, creating graphics or visuals, learning digital applications, or anything else that you can imagine taking time. Invest time into this exercise: ask colleagues or peers, ask those who have written a thesis before, and ask Google Scholar.

Standard procedure requires that you present a simple visual overview of your project timeline to complete your research proposal. It will highlight start, finish and major milestone dates.

I suggest you embellish this timeline in your year planner and populate it with the following:

- Graduation date.

- Exact start date, this is when you plan to begin.

- Exact final and draft submission dates. These are non-negotiable stakes in the ground.

- All other required submission dates, e.g., research proposal, ethical clearance, others.

- Planned holiday dates.

- Important family dates, e.g., weddings, birthdays, births and others.

- The total number of project work hours required and suggested to complete your thesis. These are based on the National Qualifications Framework (NQF) level and the credits awarded for your specific degree.

- Your personal anticipated number of project work hours per day. At least one hour a day must be dedicated to thesis-related activities, even if this is just to keep your head in the game. Aim for more hours on the weekends or public holidays.

- A week-by-week listing of planned project milestones.

This year planner and timeline must become a living and breathing part of your thesis process. Ensure it is easy to transport and is adaptable to change. Engage with it every morning and set your intentions for the day.

Calculate the notional hours using NQF levels

The number of hours required to work on your project are estimated based on the number of credits assigned to the research module you are undertaking: the NQF level.

An understanding of the NQF level of your postgraduate qualification is vital for your timeline. This must be done before you conduct your research or begin any writing of your thesis. Be proactive and research NQF levels as a matter of urgency. Here are the reasons why:

- Your specific degree earns you a precise number of credits.

- One credit is awarded for 10 notional hours of input.

- These credits indicate the number of 'notional' learning hours you need to input, over time, to be successful.

For example, if NQF level 9 (a master's degree) = 60 credits, 600 hours of input is required. In other words:

- for a research assignment that is a 60-credit module, the notional hours are 600;

- for a full master's thesis that is a 180-credit module, the notional hours are 1,800; and

- for a PhD that is a 360-credit module, the notional hours are 3,600.

Notional learning hours include all your input time: teaching contact, fieldwork, writing, planning, analysing and reflecting. In other words... everything.

How does understanding the NQL levels help?

- It provides perspective on how many hours per day you must plan to work on your research over your given timeframe.

- It highlights the degree of commitment expected to achieve the credit score.

The process

> "30 days hath September, April, June and November.
> All the rest have 31 except for February which differs in a leap year."

- Determine the number of work hours required as prescribed by the credits awarded for your degree at your university or learning institution.

- Always aim to submit a month earlier. If your thesis is due for submission on midnight of 31 October, aim to complete by 30 September because: (1) your supervisor and/or editor may come back with last minute edits; and (2) it offers you time for refinements, reflection and tweaking your closing messages. This gives you the opportunity to deliver your best work – that which will make you proud.

- Physically count each day from today until your draft submission date: for example, starting 20 March until 30 September gives you 195 days left. Remember to reduce these days by those on which you are unavailable, for example, 195-15 days family time equals 180 days. You only have 180 days left to complete.

- Next, reduce the total number of NQF hours by the hours you have already completed – assume 75. Hence 600-75 equals 525. You still have 525 hours of work.

- Divide total hours (525) still needed by number of days you have left (180). You need to find **three hours per day** to submit your project.

This number may surprise and frighten you. This is the point, because you now have some perspective on what is expected from you. This research time allocation must be added to your monthly, weekly and daily planning schedule.

Obviously, you can manipulate these hours to suit you by adding and subtracting from your daily dose. Just remember that when you lose your way, get back on track by recalculating the hours you need to do every day.

During these three-hour working stints, make sure you are completely focused and dedicated to the task at hand:

- Switch off all social media, Wi-Fi, phones, or anything distracting.

- Use a timer such as your phone, pomodoro, or whatever suits you and work for one full hour with no distractions. Coffee, toilet, must wait until the hour is over.

- That hour will be over before you know it.

- Record your hour in a spreadsheet. This is the way to keep score and measure your progress. It also acts as a powerful motivator because achievement feels good and creates momentum.

- Get up, move, toilet, stretch, make coffee, refrain from checking phone messages just yet, if possible.

- Start your timer for the next hour.

- Sit down and get to work.

Sacrifices and contracting

Let me set the scene: with a sense of achievement, success and pride at the end of your master's academic year, and with rejuvenated energy and passion, you plan your timeline for the year ahead. You are motivated, confident and enthusiastic to get going. But the thesis component of your degree is looming.

It is possible that at some stage panic sets in. It may dawn on you that you have signed up for a commitment that, apart from being extremely demanding on you, also has repercussions for your family, work, hobbies and friends, and probably requires sacrifices that you have not considered.

At this stage you may regress into either a frantic or depressive state, which may cause a needless delay to your submission and ultimately your graduation date. The consequence of this exposes you to an unnecessary and extended period of unwarranted stress. Before this happens, contemplate the following:

Contract with yourself and make the sacrifices

What are your important values and what will you do to achieve and protect them? If graduating in your chosen field is one of your top priority values, you will pull out all the stops for this achievement. I understand that finding the right balance is difficult, but you need to find the way it's going to work for you. When the going gets tough, it's important to re-connect with your highest values and make sure your degree still fits into this category.

The time required to do the work will not just fit in, so what are you willing to sacrifice? Contract with yourself on the sacrifices you are and are not willing to make during your thesis programme and list them. Golfing Wednesday afternoons with long evenings at the 19th hole, Thursday night book club with wine or Sunday picnics with the kids: what are you willing to give up? Think about this.

Identify all the support systems in your life and list them – physically write them down. For example, family, employer, clients, friends, associates, networking circles, social clubs, sporting associations, and any others you may have. Communicate with each one of them, either verbally or in writing, about your intentions for the year ahead. In other words, specify your unavailability (be explicit), the significance of this work for you, the support you require (be explicit), and the impact this will have on them until a specified date in the future. It is important to impress on your stakeholders that this is not forever, it has an end date.

"There is no success without sacrifice."[4]

Secure the necessary help

Appoint and contract with an accredited language and technical editor; preferably one that has been recommended by your institution. You may also consider transcribing and graphic design services to outsource unnecessary stress. Perhaps communicate with a mentor or coach about assistance, guidance and an accountability partner through the process. Researching and contracting these services will save you energy and distress later when the finish line is in sight.

Identify challenges

Identify any potential obstacles that could hamper your progress, for example, finances, employment opportunities, and psychological constraints such as procrastination, perfectionism, fear of failure, addictions, and others. These must be acknowledged and listed honestly because they represent a level of personal awareness that can be unpacked and managed as they surface.

Assess your technical ability and knowledge

Identify the level of computing skill you require to create your research report: your level of competency to generate an automated table of contents; the software required to draw diagrams and/or process charts to provide conceptualisation of your findings; on what language will you standardise, UK or US English? Learn how to check spelling and grammar, how to use a thesaurus, and how to find synonyms and acronyms. Create time to master the art of referencing by using digital platforms, and ensure you have secure backups. Contract with all these services, create appointments and block the time necessary to learn and use the services effectively.

Habits and the stages of change

As you well know, lasting change almost never takes place as the result of a single decision to act.[5] If you've had the 'lose weight' goal, you understand that just getting started is tough, let alone keeping up the motivation and discipline to see you through to your goal. In fact, "just doing it" before you are emotionally ready and properly prepared to tackle a particular goal may be one of the fastest ways to sabotage your success.

Science has proven that change is a progression that involves thinking, hesitating, stepping forward, stumbling backward, and, quite possibly, starting all over again. I know that the last part is hard to hear, but now that you know that this can be part of the process of lasting change, you might view your 'failure' to succeed the first time as simply part of the process.

People regularly present themselves with bad choices: take instant action or do nothing. If they act and aren't ready, half will fail. If they don't act, nothing will happen at all. The best choice? Start where you are, take steps that are appropriate for you now, no matter how small, and then keep going. Remember, no matter how small or insignificant a single small daily change seems to you, this change will produce remarkable results if repeated over time. Think of compound interest.[6] These changes become habits.

There is an increasing number of articles and books on the topic of habits. James Clear's *Atomic Habits* springs to mind. A habit, by definition, means a routine or practice performed regularly, which ultimately becomes unconscious and automatic. Mastery of anything requires practice over time, for a lifetime – it is not a once in a lifetime transformation.[7]

Similarly, writing a thesis is a marathon, not a sprint. The first part of many master's degrees normally involves lectures and examinations. Some of the habits that delivered successful exam results can be applied to your thesis, but many, such as cramming, can't. You will need to change your habits.

It helps to reframe the idea of removing bad habits into a thought of creating better habits, because this feels less like deprivation or punishment. For example, the thought of removing a bad habit of drinking coffee with sugar and milk feels like hell: no more coffee ever! But what about creating a new, better habit: drinking black coffee? This feels less life-changing and more manageable.

Imagine a real-life scenario. We convince ourselves that massive success requires massive action and we put enormous pressure on ourselves to achieve our goals. But, when we look back two years, five years, ten years, the value of good habits and the cost of bad ones becomes strikingly apparent. Never forget, one brick at a time builds the house. *Good habits make time your friend, bad habits make time your enemy*. Remember this when you embark on your academic and/or thesis project.

What is progress really like? Breakthrough moments are typically the result of many previous actions. We can so easily slide back into bad habits when the results of small habit changes seem ineffective. Do not get despondent. *It's the accumulation effect that counts*. The effects of one relapse may not be a major setback, but ongoing relapses undermine progress.

Progress is not linear. The results of our efforts are often not immediately visible. It may not be for months or years that we reap the rewards of our efforts, but your work is never wasted, it is simply stored. Keep going until you reach a tipping point, a critical threshold – one that unlocks a whole new level of performance, the full value of which will eventually become apparent. Many will think you've had overnight success, but only you will know the length of time it took to get here. *Mastery requires patience*.

Change the habit. One way to start changing your habits is to break them down into simple steps, starting off by just showing up: (1) put on your running shoes even if you don't make it out the door; (2) throw down your yoga mat even if you don't make it to the floor; (3) fill the bucket with soap and water even if you don't get to wash the car; (4) sit down at your desk, open your laptop and thesis document even if you don't write anything. When you have this small piece of your new habit mastered, build on it every day.[8]
I guarantee that if you get that thesis document open, you will engage with it and do more than stare at it.

According to Prochaska's Transtheoretical Model of Change (TTM), lasting change usually proceeds through six key stages: Precontemplation, Contemplation, Preparation, Action, Maintenance and Termination.[9] It's not always that simple, however. We can easily coast right back into preparation or contemplation if we lose our nerve, focus or steam.

Research confirms that it is necessary for individuals to believe that their considered change will make a difference to them, and perceive that the benefits outweigh the disadvantages before beginning the change process.[10, 11, 12]

For behavioural changes to become sustainable, they must enter the maintenance stage (generally, six months or more of consistent action) until they finally become subliminal. This final, ongoing stage is known as 'termination'. This implies that the change is now a permanent part of your lifestyle. Not all experts see TTM as a perfect tool, but understanding your own readiness for sustainable change may very well be a step in the right direction. What follows is a brief description of each stage.

Stage 1: Pre-contemplation

You become aware that your actions or behaviour requires change. You either change the subject or stop listening, or don't take heed. Does this ring true for you?

People in this stage may wish to change but have no tangible plans in the short-term. Why is this? They may not be fully aware of all the potential benefits, or they may feel disinclined to try because of past failed attempts or a general lack of commitment.

Weighing the pros and cons of a specific behaviour is an important component in the TTM. At first, the apparent cons outweigh the perceived pros, however as you move through the six stages, that balance shifts.

Moving from pre-contemplation to contemplation may necessitate a major life event (amongst others: a scary test result, the birth of a child, or the death of a loved one) to get you motivated to start thinking differently about change. In the meantime, recognise that just thinking about changing has potential value, and can help open your mind to new possibilities.

Stage 2: Contemplation

If your ears prick up when someone talks about the change you are contemplating, you are likely to be in stage two of TTM; you are building the confidence required to change your behaviour. However, this is the stage of ambivalence: you are thinking about taking certain action but are not quite ready or not sure how to get started. Think about academic writing.

Contemplators may think about implementing a change programme over the next six months and are open to information and research during this time. At this stage, the pros and cons of potential change feel equal, but if you can identify and amplify your unique priority values (those which are of the utmost importance to you), you could well tip this scale. In addition, visualising life after the change may prove worthwhile. Think about your graduation day.

Moving from contemplation to preparation is the right time for the low-commitment work of envisioning your better self and life: perhaps journaling or crafting a "vision board" that represents the change you'd like to accomplish.

This is also the right time to recognise the reasons why you have been contemplating change but not acted: (1) you may lack some of the necessary skills, knowledge or confidence; or (2) you may be fearful about the prospect of leaving behind familiar patterns (your comfort zone). If so, reaching out for the support of a coach, mentor or counsellor could prove meaningful. Hearing the first-person accounts of others who have already made changes can be inspiring and reassuring. Talk to other graduates.

Stage 3: Preparation

People in the preparation stage are becoming ready to act; they are more decisive, confident and committed. They are formulating a plan and may have already taken small steps. At this point, the pros of making the change clearly outweigh the cons, but there is work to be done before meaningful action can take place.

The preparation stage is all about building confidence and troubleshooting obstacles such as temptation and negative thought patterns. These weaknesses can undermine progress. This is the time to develop a contingency plan to divert the variety of challenges and temptations you are likely to face.

It's much harder to think of success strategies and temptation management techniques on the fly than it is to prepare for them in advance.

People tend to get stuck in preparation (or ricochet back and forth between it and contemplation) when they misjudge their level of readiness or impatiently jump straight to action. This can undermine their confidence and make them wary about trying again.

At this stage, I encourage people to pick a specific day on which they will officially begin their planned change. I ask them to make appropriate adjustments to their environment (e.g., their workspace, lighting, electronics, Wi-Fi, etc.), schedule the appropriate time, and assemble the support of their stakeholders.

This is also a great time to involve a coach. Alternatively, join a support group that focuses on your desired change. Now is when you want to make any other necessary arrangements. Your goal is to submit your thesis on time and graduate.

If your goal is to start a fitness plan, for example, mark your calendar with a firm date and time when you plan to begin working out, sign up for a fitness class, arrange childcare, and buy the proper shoes and workout clothes for your chosen activity.

You're in the preparation stage if you're actively gathering information, support – even gear and supplies – and feel nearly ready to take your first steps. You're feeling motivated to learn the skills that will help you be successful in making this change. You're inclined to accept the appropriate support and welcome invitations and incentives to participate in activities that will move you forward.

Moving from preparation to action: this is when you hire a coach, sign up for that class, attend a support group, buy a health club or yoga studio membership, or bring home a pamphlet for services that will help you make the change you desire. If you're determined to eat more healthily, this might be when you start clearing the junk food out of your pantry and stocking up on wholesome stuff. Any initial steps – even if they are experimental – move you that much closer to action and the sense of momentum that comes with it. Ask yourself: What, if anything, do I need to do to embrace this change in my life and be prepared for the obstacles I'm most likely to encounter?

Stage 4: Action

Now you are no longer thinking and preparing for change – you are doing the things you have set out to do and gaining confidence. This stage is where all those small steps, small choices and mini sacrifices have compounded to deliver progress.

In this phase, external support is crucial. Even if you are not comfortable asking for help, you are more likely to succeed if you do. Emotional and physical support, as well has having someone to be accountable to, will help you in the long run. It's not easy breaking old habits. Steering clear of triggers that take you off course will be a challenge. Do you need a reward for keeping to your changed behaviour? Do you need a visual reminder on your desk to keep you focused on your goal?

Look for ways to acknowledge yourself. Address new obstacles as they emerge, and reward yourself for even small successes. Action is an ongoing process, so the focus here needs to be on progress, not perfection. Let that sink in.

Moving from action to maintenance: Prochaska's model specifies that after six months of consistent action, you transition into maintenance. Getting to that point mostly involves doing whatever keeps you strong, motivated and focused. Finding ways to integrate your chosen behavioural changes into your social life and sense of identity can be a big help. During your thesis year, reframe your identity into that of "researcher". Give yourself that title and wear that hat, because despite being a learner researcher, you are doing the work and deserve the identity.

Stage 5: Maintenance

You're in the maintenance stage if for at least the past six months, you've been diligent and consistent in performing the actions you committed to as part of your desired behaviour change. They are now part of your routine, and you have avoided or overcome the obstacles that could have caused them to slip back into old behaviours. Beware of these triggers into relapse:

- Temptation
- Stress
- Crisis
- Apathy
- Boredom
- Loss of environmental or emotional support
- Frustrating plateau in progress
- Major life events – job change, romantic breakup, location change, a birth or death in the family

Whenever you fall out of action for long enough that there's a question about whether you'll be back on track tomorrow, you're probably stepping out of maintenance and back into action, preparation, or even contemplation. Do not consider this as failure, and do not make the mistake of underestimating your ability to change.

Moving from maintenance to termination: stay on the maintenance path for two years or more, rallying through stresses and setbacks, and you'll reach a point where you can't really imagine ever going back to the way things were before.

Stage 6: Termination

After two years or more in maintenance, you've now been at this long enough that it no longer seems like "behavioural change" at all; it's just the way you live – an integrated, almost effortless, part of who you are. You've likely become adept enough at the required skills that you've learnt how to apply them in new ways, perhaps to new goals in other parts of your life. You're confident enough now, in this realm, that you may even coach or mentor others in making the changes you've mastered.

Until you enter termination, hitting a wall or falling back into an earlier stage is very common, so don't be too hard on yourself. If you can identify your TTM stage, you will always know what you need to do to get back on track, recommit to your goal and make forward progress. And you'll have a clear sense of where you're headed next.

The concept of change and growth is beautifully portrayed and articulated in a poem by Portia Nelson.[13] In practice, this poem has proven to be a powerful metaphor during coaching, as it seems to resonate with clients who feel stuck in a certain stage of change. Using the poem as an assessment tool has proved invaluable to me as it has the potential to motivate and accelerate change to the next stage. The poem helped me structure my own thesis and now forms part of The Dale Method.[14]

Autobiography in Five Short Chapters

Chapter I

I walk down the street. There is a deep hole in the sidewalk. I fall in. I am lost. I am helpless. It isn't my fault. It takes forever to find a way out.

Chapter II

I walk down the same street. There is a deep hole in the sidewalk. I pretend I don't see it.

I fall in again. I can't believe I am in the same place. It still takes a long time to get out.

Chapter III

I walk down the same street. There is a deep hole in the sidewalk. I see it is still there. I still fall in – it's a habit. My eyes are open. I know where I am. It is my fault. I get out immediately.

Chapter IV

I walk down the same street. There is a deep hole in the sidewalk. I walk around it.

Chapter V

I walk down a different street.

Discipline

I've worked with many students with various degrees of motivation and discipline over the years, and this is what I've learnt. Discipline is made up of tiny daily habits and they show up for thesis work every day, whether they feel like it or not. Amongst other things:

- they celebrate the small wins;
- they make sacrifices early on;
- they ask for help from the right people;
- they thrive when they have an accountability partner;
- they make sure their workspace lends itself to productivity – no clutter or distractions;
- their planning is agile and dynamic, making it flexible to adjust when life happens;
- they plan for and schedule breaks, keeping feelings of overwhelm at bay;
- they acknowledge and manage procrastination and feelings of fear (mostly);

- they remember this is a process of learning; and
- they practice self-compassion.

Planning

The power of planning

One of the problems that students suffer from is their core belief that planning is a waste of time because they have too many other tasks on hand. This is simply not true. Planning is essential and powerful – it turns chaos into order.

- You will be in control.
- It will provide perspective.
- It will stimulate your motivation.
- It will boost your confidence.
- It will give you a roadmap to navigate going forward.
- It will reduce anxiety which in turn will reduce stress.
- It will remove that overwhelming feeling.

Slow down

Grasp five minutes to yourself (whatever works best for you) and think about the overwhelming mammoth task at hand. If this means going for a walk, taking deep breaths (this will change your nervous system), practicing mindfulness or meditation, pull yourself back into the present moment, get calm and plan.

Create perspective

Once you have formulated your timeline, identified the non-negotiable deadlines, and your year planner is populated with other important information, you have your framework. This is a clear view of the way forward – a guideline, bird's eye or helicopter view of your project ahead. Now think about how you will achieve these deadlines. This is where the real planning starts.

The dreadful thought: even though you know what you must achieve by a specified date, you do not know how to do it. Concentrate on the monthly and weekly planning.

Chunk it down

Design a mindmap or drawing or list (whatever is most appealing and creative for you) of the different chapters: typically, chapters one to five. Constantly refer to your year planner for deadlines.

- Set your monthly objectives – start from the end.

- Ask yourself the question – what does each objective mean?

- What does it really look like? Think and unpack each one.

- If you are unable to break it down, then you have no idea what step to take next.

- This will lead to procrastination.

- Do the same with weekly and daily actions plans as you go along.

- Be explicit. Very explicit.

- Semantics are powerful – do not be vague.

- Specify each book, each article, each journal and each source you need to work through – be very clear.

> When you have a plan, you know exactly what needs to be done.
>
> This knowledge builds motivation and confidence.
>
> It will create excitement to work.
>
> Because each task is easy and doable.
>
> You will feel engaged with the process.

Weekly/daily action plan

Create a list that is super specific. The worst type of action plan to manage is the one that is too vague, e.g., "Finish chapter 1". What does that mean? It is essential that you unpack exactly what "Finish chapter 1" entails, so break it down into chunks of work that are manageable and interesting. These actions must stimulate you enough to get you up and going in the morning. Ask yourself:

1. What do I want to accomplish by the end of this month?
2. What do I want to accomplish by the end of this week?
3. What do I want to accomplish by the end of today?

We tend to believe we can do more than we can, but do not be discouraged – the more you plan, the better you get.

I project manage myself as per the example below. I set major weekly tasks (I highlight in grey once they've been achieved) and then specific daily tasks (I highlight in yellow once complete). Highlighting each task gives me a sense of achievement, which is enough to keep me inspired and motivated to carry on. I use Microsoft OneNote to manage my action lists.

1.	WEEKLY ACTION PLAN
	Milestone goals due by Friday March 31st
	<ul><li>Review all existing articles and re-organise filing system</li><li>Plan meeting with supervisor</li><li>More reading on theory – autoethnographies</li><li>Read chapters 4 and 5 "Creating Autoethnographies"</li></ul>
2.	DAILY ACTION PLAN
	Monday 27th March
	<ul><li>Check ethical clearance approval today</li><li>Add reading into action plan for this week – break it into specifics</li><li>Add research work into action plan for next two weeks – specific hours</li><li>Document questions for supervisor to add to agenda for next meeting</li><li>Email to supervisor regarding next visit</li></ul>

	Tuesday 28th March
	• Research search for construct 1 – "coachability/coachability on its impact on coaching practices" etc. etc. • Read chapter 3 – *Health Behaviour and Health Education* • Read chapter 1 – *A short history of nearly everything* (Bill Bryson) • Quick overview of "Coaching for leadership"
	Wednesday 29th March
	• Existing articles search for construct 2 – "TTM/Stages of change/Self-efficacy/Decisional Balance" and other variations • Re-filing • Contact details James Prochaska? • Contact details DiClemente? • Read *Epistemological Intimacy: A Move to Autoethnography* • Schedule writing time for 45 minutes each day • Research the efficacy of committing The Writers Hour (UK) every day
	Thursday 30th March
	• 1st taped session with client • Existing articles search for construct 3 – "Professional coaching/other variations" • Complete re-filing • Read *An Autoethnography on Learning about Autoethnography.* • Book *Girl Interrupted* – bought from Loot • Complete chapter 4: Autoethnographies • Start chapter 5: Autoethnographies • Writing everyday – even if only one sentence

	Friday 31ˢᵗ March
	• Feedback from research consultant regarding chapter 1 – never happened.
	• Feedback from supervisor regarding next visit
	• Research Atlas TI
	• Complete chapter 5: Autoethnographies
	• Begin email communication with participant 1

Evaluate your action plan

- Most items are clear and specific.
- I don't feel overwhelmed when I work on my tasks.
- My monthly and weekly objectives are well-defined.
- Each task on my daily action list is explicit.
- All my deadlines are realistic.
- My work is not delayed because of fear or anxiety.
- I do not procrastinate (well, not much).
- I remove digital distractions.
- I enjoy my work.

Poor planning and under preparation

Talking about how you will spend two hours a day working on your thesis does not constitute having a plan. Many postgraduates are employed and have families and social lives to juggle. Thinking you can simply add researching and writing a thesis on top of all that is naïve and short-sighted. You will have to review your day to day, week by week activities and commitments, and adjust your schedule accordingly.

Making time for your academic work will mean making sacrifices. In my experience, the students who accept this as essential and get all their stakeholders on board with those sacrifices are the ones who submit on time, without causing animosity at home/work or succumbing to feelings of guilt. Remember, these are calculated sacrifices with a real reward at the end. Some thoughts:

- Ask your partner or spouse to take over some of the parenting responsibilities.

- Ask for accumulated/unpaid leave from your employer.

- Postpone (for now) recurring social activities.

- Say no to invitations where you can.

Part of your preparation must be directed at putting the necessary measures in place to prevent data loss. I cannot stress this enough: back your work up. Use Google Drive or other cloud storage solutions to save your work. Do not lose your writing.

Creating, negotiating and navigating a workable plan is not easy. I highly recommend engaging with a coach to assist you. In my practice, students make a PACT (Personal Action Commitment Timetable) as part of their process. The confidence they derive from having a solid and realistic plan in place has proven to be priceless.

Daily routine is essential

Start your day with a routine that works best for you. To get you going in the morning and keep you focused, this daily routine must be part of your project plan. Do not set yourself up for failure within the first week because your plan includes doing what you've tried before that did not work, e.g., waking up at 04h30 to put in two hours of thesis work. If it has not worked in the past, it's unlikely to work now.

Remember the metaphor: doing research and writing a thesis is tantamount to creating art. You are crafting your own masterpiece, and it takes time. You start with a blank canvas and come back to it time and time again until you find the right textures, colours, tools and inspiration.

Habits shape your identity

The ultimate form of intrinsic motivation is when a habit becomes a part of who you are, i.e., when your behaviour is congruent with your belief. For example, I am no longer trying to quit smoking, I am a non-smoker. This requires focusing on your identity and not on the outcome. Act like the person you believe yourself to be.

You can also become somebody you didn't believe you were, through your daily habits, e.g., a writer or researcher. As the evidence accumulates around your actions, your self-image changes. So, decide who you want to be and then move in that direction: prove it to yourself with small daily habits.

Remember this happens over time and not overnight. Our image emerges through the small things we do every day. Each time you take an action, you begin to trust yourself and hence believe in yourself.

Remember you are not perfect. There will always be votes on both sides – the good and the bad behaviour. But you don't need a unanimous vote, you only need a majority, so be kind and forgiving too. This is also a good habit.

> *"All big things come from small beginnings.*
> *The seed of every habit is a single, tiny decision.*
> *But as that decision is repeated, a habit sprouts and grows stronger.*
> *Roots entrench themselves and branches grow."*[5]

Your routine must work for you and no-one else. If you think you will get up at 05h00 each morning and go to the gym when you have been trying to do that for the past five years, forget it. Please do not try and work a routine that isn't going to work for you. It's got to be authentic, and it's got to be real. If you love drinking sweet tea, eating rusks in your gown, and reading philosophy, that's fantastic. DO IT – each morning for one hour – if you can. This is your life – do what makes you happy and encourages and energises you to get on with your day.

Keep revising your routine. Don't be scared to make changes to your routine every day if you must. It's yours, you created it, and if it's got to change, then change it. Don't feel stupid or guilty. The important thing is that it works - make your days as enjoyable as possible.

> Consider the following habits to include in your daily routine:
>
> Sleep, nutrition, exercise, inner work, laugh.

CHAPTER 5

WRITING AND EDITING

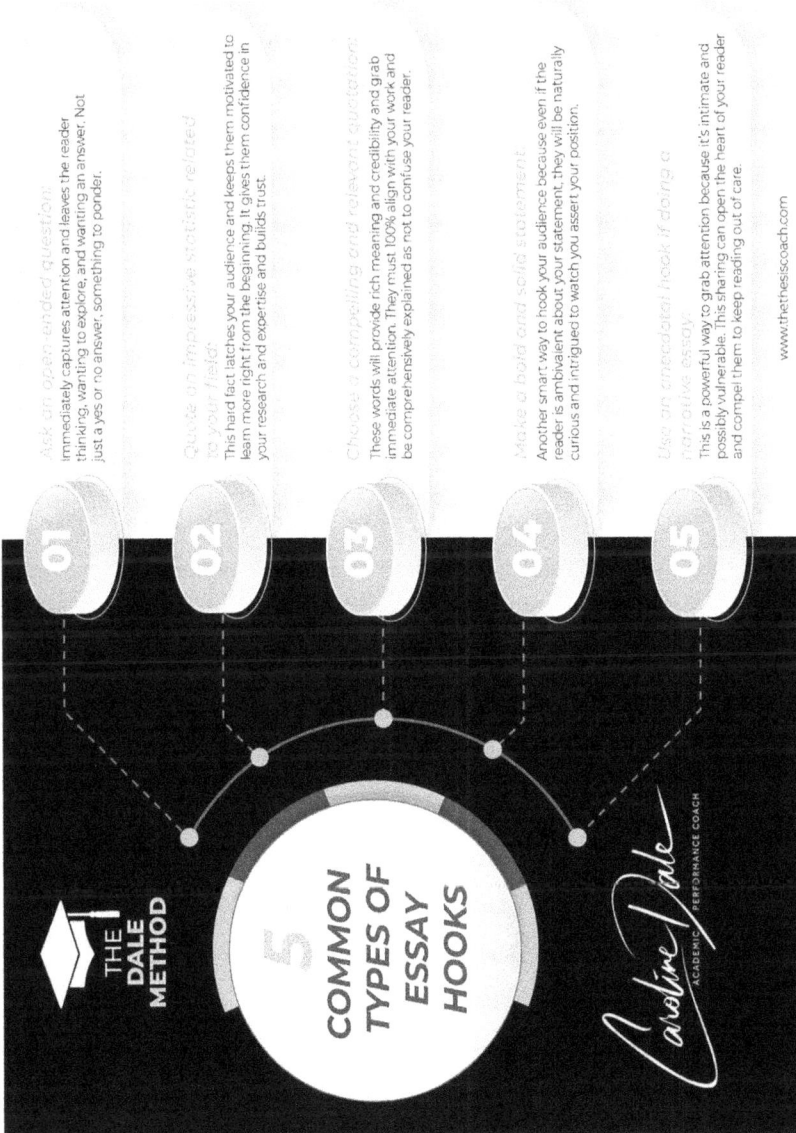

01 Ask an open-ended question

Immediately captures attention and leaves the reader thinking, wanting to explore, and wanting an answer. Not just a yes or no answer, something to ponder.

02 Quote an impressive statistic related to your field

This hard fact latches your audience and keeps them motivated to learn more right from the beginning. It gives them confidence in your research and expertise and builds trust.

03 Choose a compelling and relevant quotation

These words will provide rich meaning and credibility and grab immediate attention. They must 100% align with your work and be comprehensively explained as not to confuse your reader.

04 Make a bold and solid statement

Another smart way to hook your audience because even if the reader is ambivalent about your statement, they will be naturally curious and intrigued to watch you assert your position.

05 Use an anecdotal hook if doing a narrative essay

This is a powerful way to grab attention because it's intimate and possibly vulnerable. This sharing can open the heart of your reader and compel them to keep reading out of care.

www.thethesiscoach.com

THE DALE METHOD

5 COMMON TYPES OF ESSAY HOOKS

Caroline Dale
ACADEMIC PERFORMANCE COACH

Preparation is key

As mentioned before, my 6-phase methodology, The Dale Method, has evolved into a framework that encompasses all aspects of student challenges: timeframes, project management, habits, planning, psychological challenges, and many others that hinder student progress.

A technique to getting started is to create a thesis writing roadmap. I designed this practical technique because I find that many students haphazardly store snippets of work all over the place and this becomes deafening chaos in their minds. This chaos lends itself towards anxiety, fear, panic and an overall sense of "I don't know what I'm doing" and "I'm not going to make it".

In my experience, if you get structure into your physical working document, the chaos tends to subside. Thesis life feels lighter, and you feel in control. Plus, this is a concrete way to form a bond between yourself and this piece of work which is crucial to your success.

The thesis writing roadmap offers you a way to get started, no matter where you are in the programme. In other words, it can be used irrespective of whether you have your research topic approved or properly formulated; it picks you up from where you left off. Start working on it now.

> DOWNLOAD
>
> THESIS WRITING ROADMAP
>
> www.thethesiscoach.com

Start writing

Please remember that it is always easier to edit than to write the first draft.

> *"When you sit down to write, you can either do nothing or write, the choice is yours."*[6]

Do not make your writing complex. It is important to articulate your thoughts in uncomplicated language. The reader must not struggle with terminology or complex words. Check this by reading each sentence carefully (preferably out loud) to ensure *you* understand what you've written. Remember, this is not about impressing your reader with an elaborate narrative, it's about conveying your thoughts in a compelling way.

Sentence and paragraph structure. Sentences must be short and succinct, and it is prudent to avoid repeating words. Where suitable, cut paragraphs in half and use appropriate transition words, e.g., in addition, furthermore and in fact, to continue your flow of thought. Introduce each paragraph with a theme and exit each paragraph by introducing the next one. Create a flow.

Give reasons for all your statements. When you've made a statement ask yourself, "So what?" or "Who cares?" Then give reasons for those statements, for example: "This year of study was an incredible experience for me." What does that mean to the reader? The statement is superficial and meaningless; there is no deep thought or reflection in it. An alternative: "This year of study has taught me that learning does not happen in a linear fashion but rather in a process. It has taught me how to reflect on the problem before taking immediate action."

Explain vague words. Using the words "some", "most" or "several studies say" is too vague. Who are "some", who are "most", and what were the several studies? Explain these words either by referencing or giving a scope of reference.

Explain all diagrams and tables. These additions to your report must add value and explain your findings or themes to the reader. Do not include them just for aesthetic value.

You are the expert in your own field. If you are struggling to write, close your eyes and type what you know. If you are scared, record yourself and transcribe the recording. A first baby draft always becomes something editable.

Empower yourself. Enhance your vocabulary, learn to punctuate correctly, examine your grammar, do whatever you need to improve your writing technique. Research all the potential tools out there and identify what suits you.

Stuck on a section. If you are blocked, make a note to return to this section and move on.

It is not necessary to write in chapter order. The aim is progress before perfection.

Your workspace

This is an essential component to your literary success. Organised, inviting and comfortable is a decent start. Eliminate clutter and remove anything displeasing or distracting. Considering the significant amount of time you will spend in there, it must be a space that does not tempt stress.

> *your physical environment needs to be conducive to thinking and writing, and your thesis workspace must motivate you to act and get things done.*

Tangible inspiration. The author Roald Dahl had a strict daily writing routine, but what is most interesting is the workspace he created for himself. He physically removed himself from his home and took refuge in a small garden shed at the back of his property, which he called his writing hut. It was a tiny room with little more than an armchair and a tray table, but this was where he could allow his imagination free rein and write the most amazing stories.

Remove digital distractions. Put your devices away while you write. This means out of your line of sight and on silent. Avoid tempting rabbit hole rides on the internet or social media – these waste time and create guilt.

Craft your optimal study environment today. This is more important that you realise, so treat it as such. When you sit at your desk, you have two choices: either write or do nothing. Writing is your best option and will show measurable results – scrolling through existing work encourages you. Roald Dahl understood the value of the workspace. Does your study space serve you?

- It gets your creative juices flowing.

- It is not cluttered. You must be able to breathe. There's enough natural light by day and good lighting at night.

- Technology is solid (stable internet connection, enough plugs, screens, necessary software).

- You are comfortable at your desk: height, chair, leg space and carpet.

- Noise levels are controlled (separate room or noise cancelling headphones).

- You enjoy going to and being in this space.

- There are pictures, plants or other things around that inspire you.

Invest in the necessary tools. Aside from the room itself, it is essential that you have the necessary tools to perform the task. Any computer hardware or software is important. Invest in these. Saving money which ends up costing you time and frustration in the coming months will not be worth it. Also, invest in the time to learn your products so you don't get side-tracked with them at a later stage.

Technical considerations

In my experience, too many students get stuck in researching the literature. This process can lead to hours going down rabbit holes on the internet, ordering books from Amazon and collecting articles. Figure out when "enough is enough" and start writing.

It is vital that you set yourself up for optimal productivity and success by acquiring and mastering the necessary tools to make the job of writing a quality academic paper a reality.

Outline and technical requirements. Ensure you understand your university's specifications for margins, font, line spacing, indexing style and table titles. These will be highlighted in the module brief or available online.

Document formatting. Whatever word processing software you have chosen, you must familiarise yourself with the technology and invest the time in learning it properly. This will be the bane of your existence right through your writing process if you don't make the necessary time up front.

Referencing. You will gather many references as you write your thesis – make sure not to lose any of them in the process. Use a suitable online platform to collect and collate all your research so you can access it easily at any time. This makes referencing a whole lot easier. Mendeley/RefWorks are two of the best known referencing platforms. There are arguments as to which is better, but they both require proper tuition.

These systems allow you to store articles and books in an orderly fashion. They provide the functionality to call directly from storage into your thesis document for in-text references, and they provide for the automatic creation of your reference list based on your in-text references. Choose your referencing system as early as possible and become familiar with it. You could choose to reference manually but this will require discipline and effective management.

Language/grammar. Refer to the formal requirements and choose your word processor dictionary. It is important to differentiate between American and British English. The key is to be consistent, e.g., the "z" versus "s" difference. Even if you choose to use software to keep your grammar usage on point, you will still need an editor. Remember that editors are busy people and need contracting early in the year.

Plagiarism. You will be accessing and reading a myriad of books, journals, articles and other sources of literature to build your research case. When you use direct passages from these sources, you must paraphrase the content because the act of copying the words of another author is not allowed. It is illegal.

Paraphrasing. Read the words of another author and write it in a different way, but keep the same message as the original. It is imperative that you learn how to express something you've read into your own words to avoid plagiarism. You can effectively learn to paraphrase by following some easy steps: (1) read the passage as many times as necessary, break it up into smaller pieces, and ensure that you understand clearly what is being said (you cannot paraphrase what you don't understand); (2) remove the original passage and rewrite it from memory in your own words; and (3) compare your writing with the original and assess whether you've managed to identify the main points and reconfigure the words with the same meaning.

If you feel a direct quote is necessary because it conveys exactly what you are trying to express, you may use a direct quote in quotation marks.

Be sure to reference it correctly, which usually requires including the page number.

Graphics. How do you want to present your findings? Informative and visually appealing graphics require software and a certain level of competence. You may choose to do them yourself, which could be time consuming and expensive, or you could outsource it to a web service or a graphic designer. Investigate your options. In this respect I lean towards working smart instead of hard.

Data analysis. Once you're clear on your methodology (qualitative or quantitative), consider all your data analysis options. Again, you can opt to analyse them manually, use specific software, or contract with professional experts in the field. Invest time into researching the most relevant for you and be sure to consider the financial and time resources required to implement.

Transcription. Will you do it yourself or contract out? When working with qualitative data, the experts suggest that doing your own transcribing gives you, as the researcher, an opportunity to engage fully and deeply with the data. This is true, but because transcription is a specialist job, it could cost you more time than you have.

Editing. Select and contract with an editor/s early in the process to ensure availability when you need them. Keep in mind that it will take an editor two to three weeks to edit your thesis, depending on the page count. You must be precise about your expectations of them, i.e., language, referencing, grammar, sentence structure, or whatever you deem necessary based on what they offer. The best editors come from referrals, so ask people you know who have engaged an academic editor before.

Plagiarism detection. Upon submission, learning institutions generally run academic papers, theses and dissertations through plagiarism software. As a measure of professionalism, you can add this step to your process by making use of plagiarism detection software yourself.

Avoid reading saturation. Find out the number of references you are required to use. This sets a boundary and provides perspective on your literature search. It is not necessary to study each article and summarise it – you don't have time. Start by reading the abstract and checking the keywords, which must be relevant to your topic. Next, scan read the methodology and findings and ascertain whether they make sense to you. Finally, read suggestions for further research and see if they land with your thinking. This is not an exact science; the article must feel right. If any reading proves difficult and does not make sense, move on. Do not waste your time.

Ethical clearance. This is not an overnight process, so get to it as soon as possible. Make sure you understand the process and the systems properly. You will be unable to collect the data you need before this is approved.

Backup. Be diligent about making reliable backups of your work. If life happens and your laptop is stolen or it crashes, you'll want to have everything backed up to a cloud service as well as having a USB drive backup. Rather be safe than sorry.

Take control

Even the best laid plans veer off course. Sometimes we are forced to deal with debilitating life events or required to resolve unexpected obstacles that fall on our paths. Often these unexpected crises happen when we least expect them.

For a postgraduate student with a full-time job, a family to take care, and pending submission dates, this can wreak havoc with their plans. The most important thing is not to give up when you fall behind. Acknowledge that you've had a setback, dust yourself off, adjust your plan and pick up where you left off. It is prudent to determine the reasons for this setback and attempt to avoid a recurrence.

> It is critical that you engage with your thesis daily. This is what keeps the momentum going, provides a sense of achievement, promotes confidence, and builds motivation.

Shift your mindset from what you must do, to what you want to accomplish

If your life is being dictated by a to-do list, you will always be trying to catch up. Instead, set out three thesis goals for the day. This could be writing a section of work or creating a diagram. When you have a clear picture in your head of what you want to accomplish, you'll be more focused.

Scrutinise your daily to do list.

- How many items on it are supporting your personal and professional goals?
- How many items are supporting other people's agendas?
- Is there anything on the list that is not supporting you, but you feel "compelled" to do?

Eliminate the things that are not serving your goal to complete your thesis by saying no to invitations. Ask for help with chores and errands.

Resist distractions

It's imperative to remove any distractions that are causing you to fall behind. Phone calls, social media and email notifications that distract your attention – even if only for a minute or two – cost you in real time and consequently in getting your head back in the game.

> *"E-mail inboxes, in theory, can distract you only when you choose to open them, whereas instant messenger systems are meant to be always active – magnifying the impact of interruption."*[7]

If you come across something you need to look up, highlight, make a note and return to it later.

Don't confuse surfing the web and "researching" as productivity. Scheduled thesis working time means to focus and write. Collect your ideas and assimilate all the research you've done onto paper. There is more value in having a draft of a section that you can go back to and embellish, than walking away from a work session that has resulted in a blank page. Use a pomodoro or timer and set yourself 50 minutes. Focus, break for 10 minutes, reset 50 minutes. Record your progress.

> **READ**
> Deep Work by Cal Newport

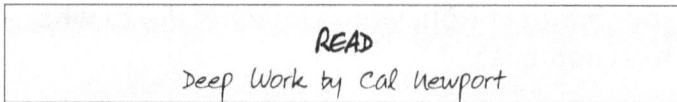

Newport[18] will help you to better understand the value and philosophy of eliminating distractions so that your time spent working is deep and productive.

Focus

Your brain can only focus on one task at a time. When you think you are multi-tasking (answering emails while working on your thesis), your brain is switching back and forth between the two different tasks. The result of multi-tasking is that your performance on both tasks is reduced, and you will feel exhausted from the effort of continuously switching back and forth.

Work smarter not harder

This sounds simple, but in practice this can be quite hard. Ensure that you choose to work in your more (naturally) productive hours. It's illogical to attempt working in the evening if you are a morning person. Block out thesis working hours in your diary and commit to them as you would for a meeting.

Ask for an extension

In exceptional circumstances, asking for an extension is fair and acceptable. Getting married (planned) and moving abroad (unplanned) in the same timeframe as doing a research project are exceptional circumstances. Dealing with these significant changes may mean that you become too far behind to catch up. It's not necessary to quit, rather ask for an extension so you don't lose what you've already done.

Find a support group or a coach

The prevailing complaint of postgraduate students is feeling isolated and losing motivation. Finding a group of people who are on the same path to discuss your problems with is valuable. It's a space to receive and give advice as well as build motivation and confidence. These discussions put your own concerns into context and build accountability to the group.

Take stock of your achievements to date and remember why you embarked on this journey in the first place. Everyone experiences setbacks. It's how you respond to these challenges that will determine your success.

CHAPTER 6

PSYCHOLOGICAL CHALLENGES

THE DALE METHOD

Managing negative thoughts

1 Accept & acknowledge this thinking as normal & difficult to avoid.

2 Avoid buying into your negative thoughts - recognize them & don't buy into them.

3 Create & nurture a "growth" / healthy mindset - you can learn & grow.

4 Develop your own rational coping statements to reinforce that which is positive as an opposite & distinct from your negative beliefs.

5 Self-help books or coaching will help you work through these & other strategies to manage negative thoughts.

Caroline Dale
ACADEMIC PERFORMANCE COACH

www.thethesiscoach.com

Mental preparedness

Anxiety, depression, trauma and other states of mind are matters of everyday life.

Anxiety is a feeling of worry, nervousness or unease, typically brought on by an imminent event or something involving uncertainty. At some stage during my thesis year, I acknowledged my own struggle with anxiety. I went through three days feeling lonely and certain that no one in the world could help me. Nobody would understand how I felt about the certain failure of my thesis project. It was going to be a disaster as I felt that all my work to date was meaningless and irrelevant. No one would be interested in the outcome of my research and thus it was a waste of time.

This period of tension manifested physically as an increase in heart rate, rise in temperature, dry mouth and extreme irritability. My behaviour was erratic and uncharacteristic, and I had a hard time communicating with anyone. I was out of control. Fortunately, by reading and forcing myself to consult with others, I eventually took control of my emotions and managed to climb out of this hole. I learnt that it is essential to acknowledge you have a problem and take the time to face it.

Have you had a similar experience? That feeling that you haven't tried hard enough? The relentless doubt: Should I be here? Am I good enough? Am I doing enough? Am I doing the right things? We turn our lives into constant comparisons. Someone always knows and does better. It never ends. You feel as if you are way behind. This is an unhealthy and destructive mindset that increases stress and anxiety and precipitates inaction.

Stress and anxiety

Undertaking a postgraduate qualification, which requires extensive research and academic writing, is a serious undertaking.

I want to take this opportunity for an honest conversation on mental preparedness. We must dispose of the idea that depression and anxiety are symptoms of weakness, or that either of these states of mind is abnormal. Have you ever met a someone who has not had a depressive symptoms? Or experienced anxiety? Me neither – we are all human.

According to the South African Depression and Anxiety Group's (SADAG) website, reporting an article in the *Sunday Times*, "South Africa is in a state of mental health crisis". Recent studies concluded the following: As many as one in six South Africans suffer from anxiety, depression or substance-use problems. This excludes the depression and anxiety triggered by crime or motor vehicle accidents.

Students experience more and more pressure to perform. Numerous studies suggest that there is a substantial annual increase of students who admit to psychological suffering during their academic programmes. Add to that growing unemployment, the high cost of living, scarcity of funds, diversity issues, political issues and social media pressures. The result? Students suffer silently with no recourse to manage their psychological challenges. This can render them feeling debilitated to the point that they will be unable to complete their tertiary education.

The buck actually stops here. The onus is on us. We are all responsible for our own mental well-being. It is up to us to educate ourselves about the signs, symptoms and strategies to manage our state of mind. The most important issue is to identify stress early. Recognise it and take the appropriate action.

Step 1: Recognise stress

Physical warning signs: fatigue, increased anxiety, insomnia, sudden weight gain/weight loss, nausea, headaches and tense muscles, amongst others.

Emotional warning signs: feeling overwhelmed, sadness, a sense of isolation/irritability, a lost desire to participate in things you used to enjoy, a lack of patience (agitation/irritability), pessimism and an inability to cope with ordinary life issues.

Cognitive warning signs: repetitive negative thoughts, irrational fears, forgetfulness, chronic worrying and an inability to concentrate on easy tasks.

Behavioural warning signs: change in eating habits or sleeping patterns, nail biting, procrastination, increased use of drugs/alcohol and a desire to be alone.

This list may provide some indicators that alert you to a potential problem caused by high levels of stress that are not being effectively managed.

Step 2: Take action

Talk to someone. Often the act of unburdening yourself from negative thoughts means they lose their importance. Hearing another person's views on your problems helps put them into perspective. Spend time with family and friends and be open with them.

Mindfulness. The practice of taking stock of how you feel at a particular moment. Identify emotions and weigh their validity to help you identify stressors early. One sure way to relieve anxiety is to write it down and express your thoughts and feelings. Another way is to focus on the positive aspects of your life.

Self-care. This means discipline on several fronts: taking breaks, getting enough quality sleep, taking care of your appearance and hygiene, eating healthily, consuming less stimulants etc., and making time for regular exercise. Belly laugh as often as you can, listen to music, chew gum, play with your pets and learn to say NO.

Breathe. Learning stress-busting breathing techniques and meditation will also help you stay calm.

Get organised. Face your work head on and plan the way forward so that you feel less overwhelmed every day.

Sensory ergonomics. Ensure that your workspace is benign, in other words, that your lighting, comfort, access to air and any other aspects enhance your mental well-being and are not toxic. Prioritise what is important to you.

Engage a coach. An academic support coach has a deep understanding of what you are going through. They will help you identify areas that need to take priority and give you more perspective on what you must be doing and how you should be doing it.

Beware of the anxiety trap

"It is a common trap that most students fall into.
The desire to be better than others.
The burning focus on goals and objectives that blinds us to our past achievements.
The insecurity about our value and relevance.
The uncertainty about the future.
The quest for perfection.
Being a student is like being in constant competition and self-doubt."
(Anonymous)

When your brain makes that comparison with someone else, your serotonin, the feel good hormone, dries up. You feel dejected and your confidence takes a knock. Instead, refer to Petersen's[19] rule four:

"Compare yourself to who you were yesterday,
not who someone else is today."[20]

During your academic/thesis years, you must be tenacious. This is a roller coaster ride, and your emotional well-being is essential to get you through. Try to strive and thrive rather than just survive. Enjoy this incredible part of your life journey and never forget to ask for help. It is there – give yourself permission to ask.

The most important thing to remember is that we all live with stress, anxiety and depression symptoms to some degree. It's not so much a mental health issue as a human condition.

Understanding negative thinking

One of the fundamental powers linked to coaching is working with problematic, self-limiting thoughts and beliefs (often distorted or irrational) that may lead to unconstructive behaviours (procrastination, not getting on with the work, etc.) and emotions. It is well-known that these can potentially block an individual's ability to function optimally.[21]

These self-limiting thoughts and beliefs (e.g., "If I fail this essay, I'm not good enough to complete the programme") may result in behaviours (quitting the programme) and emotions (self-doubt) which stimulate counterproductive emotions. In other words, people must reflect on themselves to identify irrationality and challenge negative thoughts to become more realistic and thus more balanced.[22]

Examples of negative core beliefs

If I could take you on a tour of the internal world of other postgraduate students, I would show you that self-doubt, fear, anxiety, procrastination, etc. are not unique to you. You may feel that you are the only one with these negative thoughts, feelings or behaviours, but I'm 100% certain you aren't. For example:

- "I am never going to pass this class."
- "If I can't even do well in my assignments, how am I ever going to do my thesis?"
- "I am such a loser, I'm just not clever enough."
- "How did I ever make it onto this programme? They must be crazy to have accepted me."

Or if you struggle to get your topic question right and accepted:

- "I'll never be able to understand what my supervisor is suggesting."
- "I just can't understand the revisions she wants me to make, I must be stupid."
- "I'm going to be so humiliated at my research proposal presentation."

All these result from inaction in the absence of a road map to success.

Some ways to manage this: (1) accept and acknowledge these reactions as normal and difficult to avoid; (2) stop buying into your own negative thoughts – recognise them and ignore them; (3) create and nurture a "growth" orientated "healthy" mindset – you will learn and grow; (4) develop your own coping statements to reinforce the positives as opposed to your negative beliefs; and (5) get some effective coaching.

Mastering emotions that are barriers to progress

Runaway irrational emotions

A vitally important skill in writing a thesis is the ability to master your emotions, as they cloud reason. When you develop the ability to think rationally about your real ability to deal with your academic environment, you can prepare for and respond to it with the required degree of control.

Trust your own thoughts

The psychological jargon for this process is cognitive fusion (buying in) or defusion (distrusting one's own thoughts). The way through this maze is to distance oneself from negative thoughts and use the success in your life (undergraduate degree) to establish confidence.

Replace "but" with "and"

This simple technique destroys the tendency to procrastinate: "I can write for two hours now AND go shopping later."

Fear of failure

This is one of the most prevalent and key barriers to success. Many students ask me how to manage this thought pattern, especially caused by negative and critical feedback on their work. My stock answer is always the same. Remember that you are a student and here to learn. You cannot be expected to know to be an expert in the field – not yet. Arnot[23] succinctly captures how to manage fear of failure: "use the experiences of all those rejections positively to adapt and refine ... pivot the failures; turn them into learning."

Imposter syndrome

Drs Pauline Clance and Suzanne Imes coined this term during the 1980s. Their research concluded that imposter syndrome is prevalent in persons who had overly protective and critical parents. Further research in the 2000s supported their original findings. This thought pattern is particularly likely to arise when a person starts a new job or takes on new responsibilities such as a postgraduate qualification.

The following techniques are useful in dealing with imposter syndrome and fear of failure:

- Do not compare yourself with others.

- Write down lists of important achievements you have made.

- Talk honestly and openly with your supervisor or coach.

- Cut back social media.

- Recognise that nobody is perfect.

If this list seems like too much discipline, remember that you only have to write one thesis to graduate.

Procrastination

Procrastination is a time thief and a bully. How does that influence you? Ask yourself: "Am I continually delaying or postponing taking action?"

My procrastination bully starts screaming in my head, telling me that I must really go and rearrange my bookshelf before I start working, because if I don't, I WILL become distracted while I'm working, OR, if I don't watch the last episode of Master Chef, I won't be able to concentrate. And, so, I dutifully succumb. Sadly, the domino effect takes over and can seriously side-track and blow my plans for that day.

Sound familiar? Well, don't panic! Procrastination is a complex, timeless and universal behaviour pattern and is real for many people, including myself. It is a force that side-tracks your focus and prevents you from following through on your plans. Procrastination gurus such as Tim Urban suggest that some people may have a healthy relationship with deadlines, therefore they are more able to fight off procrastination when panic sets in and they have an immediate obligation to fulfil. The problem is more hardcore when there are no short-term deadlines, e.g., in the case of a having to write a thesis or doctorate. So, what can we do about it?

Procrastination bully busters

Recognise and understand your bully when he shows up. Science has proven that your brain prefers immediate over future rewards. This means that even though your brain is cognisant of the exhilaration you will feel on graduation day, it does tend to favour feeling good right now, so your brain's desire for instant gratification can side-track you.

Be actively and consciously aware. Your future self can make plans – I will submit my thesis and graduate in December this year, but only your present self can act because s/he is living right now. So, what happens? Your present self would prefer to watch that episode of Master Chef – instant gratification – and there you find yourself back on the couch and not working. Remember, you can never catch-up time. Don't let procrastination get the better of you.

Just get your butt at your desk and commit. The problem is *starting* the work, not *doing* the work. Procrastinating is tempting but can be destroyed by action. You know that feeling – getting your active gear on in the morning and getting out of the door is way harder than the walk itself. And you know how great you feel afterwards. Writing your thesis is the same. The motivation comes after you've started the work, not before.

The consequences of your actions today DO affect your future goals. Even though your future goals seem far away, don't think that your inactivity today won't have a long-term effect. It does. Besides, rather save your "catching up" for the real emergencies that will probably cross your path.

Procrastination is a complicated and complex phenomenon from which most of us suffer. It may be worth finding out more by reading scientific papers or talking to a professional.

WATCH

Tim Urban: Inside the mind of a master procrastinator
https://www.ted.com/talks/tim_urban_inside_the_mind_of_a_master_procrastinator?referrer=playlist-talks_for_procrastinators#t-39006

Addictive behaviour

Is addictive behaviour blocking my progress?

"Addiction can be summed up by one word: MORE!
It's when you're powerless to resist MORE food,
MORE sex, MORE shopping, MORE Facebook,
MORE booze or MORE drugs."[24]

All the different types of addictive behaviours affect our emotions. For example, the gambler chases the thrill of the next bet in the hope of a big win, or a shopper desires the feeling of happiness that is triggered when they buy new shoes. Anyone can become addicted, but whatever the addiction is, it's the same process, as Dr Gabor Mate[25] clearly articulated in his short description on the psychology of addiction.

Whatever your vice, its force may be so strong that it can side-track your focus and prevent you from following through on your plans. If you can't deal with it immediately, at least start by having some understanding of what's at play in your mind and body. Suffering from an addiction is a key barrier to progress if it renders you debilitated and unable to think or work, or makes you distressed and anxious. Obviously, when your plan is to submit your thesis, becoming side-tracked and debilitated will cost you dearly.

Watch out for becoming a slave to your emotions

You know how a specific sound or smell can transport you back in time and you can literally feel the past come alive? Well, usually when this happens, tangible emotions are stirred and they manifest in your mind and body right now just as they did in the past, i.e., you feel sad, happy, angry, frustrated, or any other emotion that was real all that time ago. And all because of a simple smell or tune. During this experience your brain's limbic system is at work because it's stirring up those emotions. This is the same part of your brain that keeps you alive during an emergency; the same part of your brain that has the power to override everything you do. You need to be aware of this brain function when its power is negative.

Understand how addictive behaviour equals loss of control

When your bodily reflexes go into action, your limbic system kicks in and reacts very quickly to protect you from impending danger. These reflexes are beyond your control. This autopilot can also cause the lack of control when you're addicted to something. You need to identify this reflexive behaviour, e.g., when you just reach for that cigarette or chocolate without thinking or you reach for your mobile to check your messages or emails. Take note because when you don't give your body what it's looking for, this becomes your next hurdle.

Cravings (not only physical but dopamine cravings – checking emails etc.)

Trying to control craving may sound impossible, because if you could control your cravings, they wouldn't be an issue. But despite the disturbance cravings cause, they don't last forever – they diminish over time. Try and work through cravings by doing something different... change a habit. They will disappear. Attempt to identify, understand and take control of them.

This chapter on psychological challenges is brief and to the point. It is not intended to offer psychological support, but rather to be informative to the student who feels unable to cope with their behaviours or thoughts.

CHAPTER 7

WELL-BEING

THE DALE METHOD

A healthy mindset

is a growth mindset

Your key **thinking** revolves around **learning**

Your **intelligence is malleable** - you can become more clever through hard work and **persistence**

You **observe and evaluate** your performance with **no judgment**

Success and **positive feedback** mean you're learning / failure and **negative feedback** mean **you're learning**

You are more motivated to learn and therefore achieve more academically because **your academic disappointments have no power over you** – you know you are learning - this is why you are at a learning institution.

Self-care

An integral part of your strategy for success, and a part of your thesis schedule, is to find time to take care of yourself. To manage stress and anxiety, you need and deserve time for rest, exercise, relaxation and enjoyment. Your thesis is only one aspect of your life and is finite – it will come to an end. Ensure that self-care features as an additional priority to your thesis goals. Give yourself permission and do not allow guilt to derail you. Self-care should be a way of life; a philosophy in which you value the quality of life.

Students often procrastinate in an unhealthy way by overindulging in things that are easy to do, such as binge-watching YouTube or Netflix. These activities may bring relief and some level of relaxation, but do not recharge your energy or motivation and are likely to lead to feelings of guilt. Find restorative activities that give you pleasure and energy.

There will be times during your thesis project when you decide that there is no time for self-care. You will dismiss your own needs for care and enjoyment and tell yourself that you will find time once your thesis is submitted. These thoughts and actions will mobilise bad habits for the future, because life after your thesis will continue to present challenges. Other major projects like career, family and health will arise and the habits learnt of delaying self-care, exercise and relaxation will remain. Self-care is vital to life, especially during your thesis year.

> *"It takes ten times as long to put yourself back together as it does to fall apart."*[26]

You are on a thesis marathon. No athlete planning to run an ultra-marathon would train every day without rest. They know that optimal performance requires including healthy rest, good nutrition, and taking extra care of their bodies and minds. The risks of injury or illness through exhaustion is too high and will end in suboptimal performance. This analogy proves that over-taxing your brain without meaningful rest time will not ensure optimal academic performance.

I understand the pressure of writing a thesis. I also understand the guilt when you decide to allow yourself a little time off. The reality is that you will be of no help to yourself when burnout takes over. Plan purposeful breaks that are guaranteed to launch you into productivity and not guilt or procrastination.

Develop your own regular self-care practices

Schedule self-care into your routine. Sleep, tidy your room, eat breakfast, drink more water and have a bedtime dop (one only). Build a daily self-care routine and stick to it. This could include practices such as mediation, mindfulness, reading, stretching, yoga, massage, exercise, reflective writing, etc. Perhaps even find an app that can measure these activities for you – there's nothing like the feeling of achievement. It's crucial to try to be with yourself and engage in restorative practices, even if only for a short time each day or week.

Poet May Sarton on the importance of rest:

> *"I always forget how important the empty days are, how important it may be sometimes not to expect to produce anything, even a few lines in a journal. A day when one has not pushed oneself to the limit seems a damaged, damaging day, a sinful day. Not so! The most valuable thing one can do for the psyche, occasionally, is to let it rest, wander, live in the changing light of a room."*

Know the value of sleep. Many people don't understand the value of sleep. Your physical, cognitive and emotional performance are all affected by the quality of your sleep. I understand that sometimes one needs to work later into the night to meet a deadline, but this should certainly not become an ongoing habit. If you are proactive and plan your thesis year well, it would be prudent to commit to a healthy sleep pattern. "Millions in the world are chronically sleep deprived and suffering the deleterious effects of getting low quality sleep."[27]

Get more sunlight. Sleep is heavily impacted by the amount of sunlight you are exposed to during the day. In addition to the well-known benefits of vitamin D exposure, science proves that sunlight affects your circadian rhythm which significantly improves your quality of sleep.[28] As a postgraduate student, you need this sleep for energy and cognitive function.

READ

Sleep Smarter

Shawn Stevenson

Nutrition. My simple diet mantra, from Professor De Villiers in his book *Blueprint for Better Health*, is: "It's not what you eat that counts, it's what you don't eat that counts." With the countless philosophies on eating plans available, you will know what your preferences are. Strive to include as much nutrition in your daily diet as possible, without deprivation of some "nice stuff". Understand that nutrition feeds your brain and affects your cognitive functioning.

Make time for personal development. Spiritual, mental or cognitive – anything that keeps you physically and mentally in balance.

Visualise your graduation day. You play many roles in your life (wife, husband, partner, girlfriend), but during this phase you are a postgraduate student researcher. This is who you are. Your vision of who you are becoming must motivate and inspire you. Never forget why you ventured into this role in the first place. You had a vision. Remember it.

Self-doubt is inevitable; ignore it. There will be a point where you feel that you should never have embarked on this journey in the first place. Impostor syndrome, fear of failure, self-doubt, procrastination and others are commonplace amongst people tackling big goals, and are especially true for many postgraduate students. Acknowledge these thoughts, which are unlikely to be true, for what they are. Your supervisor will alert you to any problems in your thinking or content. Keep going and give it your best.

Let go of perfection. Many overachievers develop perfectionist tendencies at a young age, which is a habit that is hard to break as you mature and take on more responsibilities. It's good to get some perspective and realise that perfection may be out of reach. If you know you have perfectionistic tendencies, then try and reframe and focus on progress as a measure of success. Avoid burn out and rid yourself of the need to be perfect.

Holiday stress. Don't allow tiredness, burn out and loss of energy to deplete your self-esteem and confidence levels during holidays. There is no energy in the pit of low self-esteem to build confidence and keep yourself going.

Don't take yourself too seriously. We are unique human beings and have our own insecurities, peculiarities and possibly strange ways of dealing with people and things. Ignore or get over small irritations quickly; they're not worth your energy.

When you stop working, STOP working. You do not have to answer every e-mail or text message immediately. When you leave your place of employment or your home desk, consciously shift your attention away from the office. Be cognisant of your surroundings on your drive home and enjoy the ride. Be present with your family when your workday is over. Leave your work at work and your thesis at your desk. You need time to be with yourself and those you love.

De-compress. Dance naked in the rain, have that bubble bath, get messy, swim in the ocean, make some noise and sing at the top of your voice, or dance to your favourite tunes.

Belly laugh every day. This is good for the soul.

Don't stop believing. Read the opportunities in every setback and challenge. No success comes without falling and getting up again. Fail spectacularly. That way you learn.

These practices will keep you resilient and help you to manage stress and maintain focus:

- Regular weekly exercise will combat tension and anxiety.

- Eating well by choosing nutritious foods over junk food will sustain and replenish your energy levels.

- Good quality 8-hour sleep every night will literally keep you sane and ensure that all your bodily processes work as they must.

- Mindfulness keeps you present, living in the moment and connected to those from whom you receive daily support.

Sitting is the new smoking

When we take up exercise and eat more healthily, we are often driven by improving our bodies, losing the extra kilograms, or improving flexibility. We omit to think about the beneficial effects of physical activity and what we eat on our brains. Regular cardio exercise along with the incorporation of memory boosting food will elevate your mood and improve your cognitive function.

Researchers have found that regular aerobic exercise, the kind that gets your heart and lungs working, appears to boost an area of the brain called the hippocampus (responsible for verbal memory and learning).

Exercise helps memory and thinking through both direct and indirect means. The direct benefits of exercise come from its ability to reduce insulin resistance and inflammation. Simultaneously, exercise stimulates the release of certain chemicals in the brain. These chemicals affect the health of brain cells, the growth of new blood vessels in the brain, and the abundance and survival of new brain cells.

Indirectly, exercise improves mood and sleep which reduces stress and anxiety. As you may well have experienced in your own life, when you are stressed, eating poorly and in a bad mood, your "thinking" work suffers.

Many studies have suggested that the parts of the brain that control thinking and memory (the prefrontal cortex and medial temporal cortex) have greater volume in people who exercise versus people who don't. This means we can increase our brain capacity in areas that are responsible for rational thinking and ideas by simply exerting ourselves to the point that our heart rate increases and causes us to break a sweat.

Human beings are not genetically programmed to live in a state of idleness and lethargy. If we do, our brains pay a high price, both in the short- and long-term. The neurological benefits of physical activity that will be of interest to a student include the following:

- Decreased stress.

- Improved processing and managing emotions.

- Euphoria (short-term).

- Increased energy, focus and attention.

- Improved memory.

- Improved blood circulation.

- Decreased 'brain fog'.

A growth versus a fixed mindset

Fixed mindset

Dr Dweck coined the terms fixed mindset and growth mindset to describe the underlying beliefs people have about learning and intelligence.[29] The way you view what you do and the outcome of your effort will immediately reveal whether your predominant mindset is fixed, or one of growth. Are you only results-driven, seeing total success as the only acceptable result? Does a major setback seem like the end of the road? Do you believe that if you were meant for the task (thesis writing) it should come easier? Have you thought about quitting because it's just too hard? Then there's a strong case to be made that you're stuck in a fixed mindset.

This is not a good place to be, and in many ways, it's a flavour of self-sabotage that happens on an unconscious level. We are all susceptible, and we all succumb to the fixed mindset at times. In my experience, receiving less than my personal expected grade for a piece of work left me feeling inadequate and a failure. I reeled from some of the remarks, criticisms, suggestions and red scratches through my work. On some occasions I even considering giving up because I felt I wasn't good enough. I had to remind myself that I was there to learn.

The fixed mindset is obsessed with performance. It believes that intelligence, creative talent, and cognitive skills are gifts and just something you have, not assets that you can grow and develop. This mindset also believes that negative feedback, even constructive feedback, insinuates that you are a failure. This leads to low motivation, which causes you to procrastinate and suffer feelings of inadequacy and fear.

> *"Those with a healthy mindset are flexible. They do not get stuck or bogged down by rigid thinking or compulsions. They are open to new ideas and are capable of change when appropriate. They are also resilient. They understand that bad things happen to all of us, but the healthy ones bounce back as required, repeatedly."[30]*

The good news is that neuroscience has shown us that the brain is a malleable organ; it can adapt to new challenges and learn new skills. This means you can shift your mindset from a fixed state to one of growth.

Shift to a growth mindset

Awareness. Now that you are aware of how self-limiting your thoughts can be, you can change the voice in your head and give it a fresh narrative to follow.

Focus on learning, not performance. Ask yourself these questions: What can I learn? Who can I ask for help? What else can I do?

Re-identify your original goals. In other words, ask yourself why you are at this learning institution? Why are you doing this thesis? What was your original motivation? Have you disengaged and lost sight of the purpose?

Remember how you love to learn. You have been doing it all your life – literally from birth. Give yourself time and space to explore. Don't set standards, but rather view progress as the ultimate victory. This might sound somewhat trivial, but the truth is, if you think of every major success story, nothing ever came easy, and the one thing they all have in common is persistence and tenacity. Persistence despite obstacles. Despite rejection. Despite criticism. If there ever was a time to adopt an attitude of pig-headed persistence, the time is now.

Tame your mind. The best thinking happens when your mind is calm; that's when deep focus is easy. Add good quality sleep, regular exercise, a decent diet and a mindful approach to life and the difference it makes to how you view setbacks will be a real game changer.

Access your working memory. Your brain draws from your body – it needs sleep, exercise and good nutrition to work optimally. According to Cal Newport, the author of *Deep Work*, we don't give our brains enough idle time to allow it to solve problems and come up with brilliant ideas. So, stop scrolling on your phone after being bored for a minute and think twice about what media you are allowing your brain to consume.

Dealing with traumatic life events

Psychologists have identified death/birth, divorce, moving house and a change in financial circumstances as dominant stress-inducing life events. During the past two years, we can add living through a pandemic to this list. On a superficial level, working from home seems like the perfect time to knuckle down and get the writing done, but this comes with its own set of challenges: spouses and children at home, home-schooling, financial stress – to name just a few. If you experience a traumatic turn of events in your life do not assume you can simply stick to your original plan – that is just setting yourself up for failure. Instead, review and adjust your plan. Speak to your supervisor and acknowledge the problems you are experiencing. The quicker you adjust your strategy, the better your chance of success.

CHAPTER 8

ACHIEVEMENT AND SUCCESS

#TopTips

To help you deliver a polished thesis

1. Formatting & Style

CONSISTENCY IS CRUCIAL

- Consistent styling of bullet markers.
- Consistent heading structure.
- Consistent letter/number references.
- Consistent line spacing/fonts aligned with formatting & style requirements.

2. Special pages

Ensure ALL special pages at the beginning of your report are in line with style guide provided.

3. Final touches

BE A PERFECTIONIST

- References must be accurate.
- Have you met the word/page count requirements?
- Are all diagrams correctly and consistently named?
- Are you proud to put your name on your work?

Definition of success

Everyone has a unique vision for their own success. We all know that perseverance can be challenging in the face of obstacles, but if you remember your reasons for undertaking this degree and remind yourself of the master plan, you have defined what success looks like for you in the long-term.

> *"The meaning of success is different for each person. You may not fit into other people's definition of success, but you can give yourself permission to be OK with that. Success is an individual concept. Here's the exciting part: you get to define and design your own success, which will become the blueprint for you to follow throughout your life. Developing your own success blueprint also means that you get to create success on your own terms."*[31]

As obstacles arise, you must take full responsibility to stay on course. Ask yourself:

- What obstacles prevent me from achieving my desired level of success?
- How will removing these obstacles help me to achieve this?
- How can I hold myself accountable during the process?
- What action steps can I take to help me achieve more?

Once you define the action steps that are required to achieve more and understand what's holding you back, you can begin to make progress.

Taking time to define success means making a conscious decision to shift from a fixed mindset to one of growth. Acknowledge that there will be setbacks, but that you have the tenacity to overcome and learn from them. A healthy definition of success is one that contemplates the joy of the journey and the purpose that extends beyond the end goal – the master plan. How thrilling will it be to finally stand on that graduation stage?

In my experience as an academic performance coach, I've seen clients reach their goals in different ways, but it all begins with their expectations. If you expect it to be a slog for 12 long months, it will be, but if you are prepared to work on your own definition of success before you start, you'll find yourself more focused and motivated to get started.

Tips for achieving success

- Effective planning.

- Being busy does not necessary mean being productive, so prioritise.[32]

- Remind yourself daily that your graduation is a priority.

- Be realistic about your time. Do not set yourself up for failure.

- Be realistic about your goals. If you don't achieve a distinction does that really mean you've failed?

- Be flexible. Plan for the unforeseen and always build a buffer into your timelines. If you do this effectively, an unforeseen life or work event will only be a minor setback and not a major crisis.

- Engage with your thesis every day to develop a healthy relationship with your work.

- Celebrate the small victories. Finished writing that chapter? Crack open the bubbly!

Be proactive

Proactivity was introduced as a scientific concept about 25 years ago and has been investigated under several different labels, including 'personal initiative'. An increasing number of studies show the beneficial effects of different types of proactive behaviour at work for individuals, work teams and organisations. These positive effects have been found for several different outcomes, including work performance, career success and individual well-being, all of which are relevant to students working towards academic performance and success.

When your thesis project commences, be proactive and start your journey towards academic success. Take immediate action to create a sense of control before your stress levels rise and anxiety creeps in.

Over the past three years, I have mentored and coached almost 100 postgraduate students. Without a doubt, those who chose to be proactive at the beginning of the year submitted good work on time and, equally importantly, enjoyed the project. Whoever or whatever you choose (online courses, mentor, coach, triad, alumni, friend or family support), make a strategic choice to be proactive and discover the thrill and excitement of achievement and success.

Benefits of being proactive

Road map the future. Proactive individuals plan for and build the future they want without waiting on external forces to determine which direction they should go in. Acting proactively means that you are forward-looking. You've identified that there's work to be done and mechanisms to be put in place because you're aiming to deliver the best academic work you can.

Alleviate problems or issues before they happen. You can uncover potential problems or conflict and minimise your exposure to it. For instance, if you know you will need a certain software programme for your data handling, you can schedule the time to learn how to use the application effectively.

Be more prepared. You are thinking about what could happen today to avoid chaos tomorrow. You have a backup plan so that unforeseen events and circumstances are only setbacks and not failures.

Save time and money. You are putting in the effort to save time and money by preparing now instead of at the last minute. Booking an editor or other potential services early is a good example of this.

Peace of mind. You are comfortable with where you are and where you are going because you have an idea of what is coming.

Accountability

Accountability is vital to achieving life-changing goals. The question is, why?

While there are numerous definitions of "accountability", most explanations point to one's willingness to accept responsibility for one's actions. Other explanations reference the words 'blame', 'victim', 'liability' and 'answerability'. While there is some truth in these heavily emotive words, simply put, being accountable is doing what you say you will do; staying true to your word by following through on your commitments and (here's the bull's eye) showing up.

It makes sense for me to think of it in its purest form: accountability is a combination of an obligation + an action + a specified other person. Showing up for the specified other person is the crux of true accountability. It's more than just getting the job done, it's about having a dedicated individual care about whether you're achieving your goals.

How to contextualise accountability

Having a "specified other" in the accountability equation means that accountability, like all meaningful relationships, is a two-way street. How do I hold myself accountable to my clients, and how do they hold me accountable?

In my own context as Caroline Dale, the Thesis Coach, my clients are at the heart of my profession. On the one hand, I recognise that my service must be delivered with punctuality, professionalism and vigour. I am accountable to them by showing up as a coach in good spirits, with an open ear, keeping them accountable for delivery, and being fully present to help them achieve their objectives. I am their accountability partner. On the other hand, I hold each client accountable for sharing their story and for showing up with an open mind, a healthy attitude towards learning and a commitment to achieving success. Mutual respect and honesty are non-negotiable.

Accountability should be present in all the important areas of one's life. It is essential that the teams that support my business hold me accountable to give them clear and precise instructions. And, in turn, I hold them accountable for delivering quality work, on time, and with passion and thoughtfulness. It is essential that we commit to meet regularly, whether face-to-face or virtually, to ensure that mutually agreed-upon deliberate actions are tracked and monitored and that we hold each other accountable – professionally and personally.

The Association for Talent Development (ATD) conducted a study on accountability and found that you have a 65% chance of completing a goal if you commit to someone. If you have a specific accountability appointment with a person to whom you have committed, you will increase your chance of success to up to 95%.

Why does being accountable to a coach work?

The two factors that effectively help people achieve their goals are incentives and accountability. A coach fulfils the latter part of the equation because as human beings, we are wired to please others. That's why being accountable to only oneself is simply not enough; we need consequences and recognition.

Key benefits

Motivation. Having a set appointment with your coach on a regular basis to report back on your action list delivers the necessary motivation for further effort. Clear targets and deadlines provide a healthy amount of pressure to succeed. If you don't follow through, you'll have to face your accountability partner and admit failure – not an easy task for the ego. Setting a specific appointment or meeting time also creates a social expectation, which is another powerful driver to keep you focused.

Systems. Formulate and maintain structures, processes and systems to measure and record your progress. The routine of delivering on your promises will seal the thrill of achievement and success.

Greater clarity and direction. Identifying explicit outcomes that are crucially important helps you to capture better quality opportunities. It also helps you to say 'no' to things that don't support these outcomes. Everything else is eliminated, delegated or outsourced. This accountability focus will keep you on track and productive.[33]

> *READ*
>
> Essentialism: The Disciplined Pursuit of Less
> Greg McKeown

Becoming results focused. When you are accountable to achieve a specific, measurable result, you become more intentional and focused about where to spend your time. If you are reporting results to an accountability partner, your time and energy is focused on delivery. You will find that your morale, momentum and motivation will flourish.

Managing your time effectively. We have only 24 hours in a day. When we become accountable for delivering certain results, we start managing our time effectively; we take ownership of our hours by setting clear boundaries, saying no more frequently, and exerting more influence over our own schedules.

Manage procrastination. One of the key benefits of working with a coach is managing procrastination. If left unchecked, it can leave you feeling stuck and trapped for days, weeks or even months. This is a problem that everyone faces from time to time – you are not alone. Learning to recognise and manage procrastination is vital in one's attempts to alleviate the doom and gloom that it leaves in its wake.

Setting achievable and realistic goals. It is easy to set goals but unless they are unambiguous, measurable and have a deadline, they often fall by the wayside. A coach can help you set goals that matter to you and create a plan and path to achieve them, which will transform how you think and work. Regular check-ins ensure you stay focused and on track.

Action plan. When obstacles or challenges occur, the coach in your corner will help you create an action plan to move forward. A continual review of performance and progress and tweaking efficiency levels will keep you accountable to the results that are meaningful to you.

Sign a PACT with yourself. (P)ersonal, (A)ction, (C)ommitment, (T)imetable. By definition, a PACT is an agreement between two people, however in my opinion, one must aim to make a PACT with oneself too: one that is clear and meaningful. I have deliberately assigned the words 'personal', 'action', 'commitment' and 'timetable' to the acronym to make the word PACT explicit and personal.

This is a commitment contract – a binding agreement you sign with yourself to ensure that you follow through with your goals. Remember to keep timeframes flexible because unforeseen challenges can force you to veer off track. This is not failure, it is simply an obstacle to step over and resume your plan.

In my experience as a coach, when you make people accountable for their actions, you're effectively teaching them to value their work. Having someone to share the journey, keep you motivated, be your cheerleader and crack the whip makes all the difference.

Motivation

What motivates us? What stops us from getting on with what we know we really want to do? This is an ongoing life question. My views on motivation keep me researching and thinking about how fear and confidence, associated with my own abilities, are at the forefront of my own personal motivation levels.

For example, when my immediate workload and/or trying to balance my personal and work life feels overwhelming and too much (this is the trigger), I respond by feeling afraid and out of control (my emotional response). When this happens, I have an innate tendency to speed up my activity (my behavioural response). This causes me to rush around like a crazy person trying to get things done. I feel like I must prove my own self-worth so I hide behind my own "busyness" to stop taking action about whatever it is I'm afraid of doing, like writing my next assignment, thinking about my research methodology, or considering my next academic article.

Fear is my trigger. My definitive physiological (increased heart rate and sweaty palms) and psychological responses (anxiety spirals out of control) cause me to think that everything I'm doing is worthless and many more negative thoughts creep into my thinking. In addition, I think impending thoughts of doom about my own self-worth and my lack of ability; this is lack of confidence speaking.

When I get here, I know it is time to SLOW DOWN. I know I need to think smaller. I need to take what feels overwhelming, unpack it and figure out the smaller, more manageable ways of dealing with my workload. This puts me back in control.

When you get to this stage of your studies, how are you going to slow down and start to think smaller? Take five minutes and do what works best for you: (1) take five deep breaths to calm your nervous system; (2)

go for a walk; (3) meditate. Whatever you do, pull yourself back into the present moment.

Guilt and fear are the two most debilitating emotions; guilt for something you have already done (which you can't change) and fear about something in the future (which you can't change). So, get back into the present moment and get a grip of your emotions – take control of yourself.

Alignment with your priorities and goals and having a steadfast plan in place must stimulate your motivation and boost your confidence whilst calming your anxiety by removing overwhelming feelings.

Recall any goal that you set for yourself in the past which you achieved successfully. I'm willing to bet that if you think about that time in your life, you'll remember how determined you felt. You knew that it was up to you to make the changes necessary to achieve your goal and you pig-headedly believed you could and would do it. And then you did. Psychologists call this ability to motivate yourself to make significant changes in your life, 'self-determination.'

Confidence and motivation

Self-doubt often manifests as imposter syndrome during the thesis year, usually when you feel that you are too far behind to catch up and finish on time. While it is 'normal' to have doubts, if your state of mind is so negative that it's debilitating, you must immediately talk to your coach or supervisor to gain some perspective and help you navigate the crisis to get back on track. You would not be in the postgraduate programme if the institution and its staff did not believe you could pass.

Motivation is another common problem. Performing research and writing the necessary reports is a discipline. Believe me when I say, motivation is your fickle friend who only shows up when the sun is shining. You must learn this important fact: do not rely on motivation to get you to sit down and put in the hours. 'Just sit down in your chair and start writing.'

As well as being motivated to pass your course, you need to be disciplined. Show up for thesis writing every day, as you promised yourself, and success will follow, I promise you.

What motivates us?

We are motivated intrinsically and extrinsically. Intrinsic motivation means we do things because we want to – they make us happy and satisfy us on a deep level. No external reward is necessary. Extrinsic, or external motivation, is the age-old carrot or stick. We do things because we feel we must do them. External motivation rewards us with money or recognition – or because if we don't do or perform the actions, the consequences will be detrimental.

While both types of motivation are powerful and often are at work at the same time, internal motivation is a far more powerful and long-lasting driver for success. Intrinsic motivation is also the foundation of self-determination, which is the major factor in our ability to make decisions that have a positive effect on our lives.

What is self-determination?

Simply put, self-determination is a person's ability to be autonomous, that is, to make choices and manage your own life. Being self-determined and feeling like you have the autonomy and freedom to make choices that shape your destiny are important for your well-being.

When you pursue things that are intrinsically motivated, that are "aligned with your top priority values and goals",[34] you will feel happier and more capable of making good choices. It will also have an impact on motivation – people feel more motivated to act when they feel confident that what they do will influence the outcome.

How to improve self-determination

Believe you have control over your own life. It is up to you. What you do will influence the outcomes. When you are confronted with challenges, believe you can overcome them through diligence, good choices and hard work.

Be self-motivated. Remove all ideas of external rewards or punishments from your mind-set. Be single-minded in taking actions that will serve your master plan.

Take responsibility for your choices and behaviours. This means taking credit for successes as well as acknowledging failure as your own, without blaming anything or anyone else. Be accountable, but never forget that failure is part of the learning process.

Work on being more self-aware and improving certain skills. Improving self-awareness, decision-making skills and goal-setting abilities will give you the confidence to be autonomous.

Believe in the power of planning. This will give you a structure, keep you in control, maintain your motivation, and keep anxiety and procrastination at bay.

Get a coach. Autonomy is one of the most fierce and potent needs of human beings,[35] and this is where having a coach will make the most impact in your life. Do you have the right level of motivation and the right level of confidence? Do you have the strategies to get past the obstacles that get in the way of taking action? You need energy plus conviction plus structure to develop and maintain motivation.

In addition, a competent coach will draw out your innate ability to be autonomous. They will guide you on how to manage your challenges and help you dig deep to answer the crucial, intrinsically motivating question: What does your desired outcome (to complete your thesis) really mean to you? Nothing will make you feel more committed, passionate and satisfied about your goal ahead than feeling in control and intrinsically motivated.

Your time to shine

During the last month of your project, you will feel that you've had enough. You will be exhausted and stressed. While some might convince themselves that they have done all they can and slack off, students who push through and work on polishing their thesis are the ones who take their work from good to great, and possibly distinction.

I remember the last week of my thesis work with precise clarity – it was equal parts of wonder and pain. Being a perfectionist and somewhat OCD, this period was backbreaking. I pulled 24-hour stunts at my desk: cross-checking references; tweaking sentences; moving paragraphs to refine the flow; improving the quality of diagrams (even if they had to be redone); using thesaurus and synonym searches to improve grammar; checking for punctuation; searching for "z" words; researching the use of colons, semi-colons, dashes and hyphens; and asking for help, even if just to make coffee.

It was strenuous, my shoulders and body ached, but I soldiered on till the bitter end. I was like the proverbial dog with a bone. That's the nature of the beast... my nature. Some may suggest that I'm stark raving mad, but I personally believe that's how I achieved a distinction. Despite the backbreak, this time was also exciting because this is when I was able to stand back and behave like an editor: it is always easier to edit than to write from scratch.

My point here is don't stop now, keep your momentum alive and push your limits. The result will be one of your proudest moments. I did the best work of which I was capable at the time, and I remain proud of the outcome.

Polish your thesis

In my experience as an academic performance coach, it's this time of year that calls for the all-important final checks; making sure your work is perfect and ready to be submitted as a professional body of work.

This is your masterpiece – the art you've been creating from an empty canvas since day one and a piece of work of which you must be supremely proud. Your blood, sweat and tears have produced this outcome. Don't give up now – tweak it until the end.

> *"This is your masterpiece and it's almost ready to be revealed.*
> *Day one was a blank canvas, today there is full colour.*
> *Blood, sweat, and tears were the hidden drivers in your painting palette.*
> *Your supervisor, family and coach were the brushes that pushed you to paint.*
> *The final glow must be added.*
> *This is your time to shine."* (Caroline Dale)

For this exercise, I suggest you print out the entire research report and take out your red pen. Please note, this checklist is just a guide and therefore not exhaustive. During this editing process, constantly look out for amendments to improve your grammar, punctuation or flow. And don't forget to ask for help from anyone willing to read a chapter.

☑ Checklist

- Your table of contents (TOC) numbering is consistent with the rest of the document.

- All diagrams and tables are correctly named and referenced.

- Consistent bullet point markers (round or square).

- Consistent spelling rules for US or British English, e.g., the use of 's' or 'z' in places.

- When you describe diagrams, ensure the explanation matches the diagram in terms of numeric or alpha labels.

- Heading structures and formatting is correct and in line with the style guide provided.

- Structure for tables, appendices, acronyms, abbreviations and figures are in line with the style guide provided.

- Do you have the correct page/word count for successful submission?

- Make sure the number of in-text references matches the number in your reference list.

- Your references must be accurate and support the citation style required.

Now is not the time to sabotage all the effort you've already put in, now is your time to shine.

Mental strength

Here are some ways you can build up your mental strength and actively put tenacity into practice. Remember that you are in control. One of my favourite Stoic philosophy quotes is:

> "The chief task in life is simply this: to identify and separate matters so that I can say clearly to myself which are externals not under my control, and which have to do with the choices I actually control."[36]

Put aside that which you are unable to impact right now. Mental strength is like muscle strength – no one has an unlimited supply, so why waste your energy on things you can't control?

See past mistakes as valuable training and nothing more. Do not hyper focus on the parts of the thesis journey that went wrong. Make a conscious effort to frame what went wrong and identify the lesson learnt. Then move on.

Celebrate the success of others. If someone else shines it does not detract from your ability to shine. Resentment sucks up a massive amount of mental energy, which would be better applied elsewhere.

Create a tangible reminder. This could be a vision board or a sticky note on your computer. Mental fatigue makes us take the easy way out – even though the easy way may take us the wrong way. Tangible reminders go a long way to help us resist the impulse of making choices that take us from the path towards our goal.

The question of a thesis coach

From my own experience as a thesis coach, I have found that too many postgraduate candidates are suffering either prolonged periods of stress related to submission delays or real challenges to face the task at hand.

Would a thesis coach help?

A thesis coach focuses on postgraduate students – specifically those navigating the thesis phase of their qualification. They provide the following services through individual one-on-one coaching sessions:

- Coaching to evaluate the client's highest priority values to understand and determine the level of commitment to their topic choice. Usually, a specific highest value drives the topic choice, which in turn drives and motivates the process towards thesis completion.

- Coaching to incorporate proven and practical project management techniques for goal setting and planning. This will support the client to establish control over their own process and to manage their work/life/thesis balance.

- Coaching to ascertain the most effective routine/s for the client to manage their own discipline and hence their motivation.

- Coaching to support the client through unpacking and managing common psychological challenges that cause barriers to achieve objectives, e.g., procrastination, fear of failure, self-doubt, addictive behaviour and obsession with perfection, amongst others.

- Coaching to highlight motivational techniques to stimulate high quality work and progress towards completion.

- Coaching to provide a combination of coaching, mentoring and teaching depending on the unique requirements of the client.

In summary, this is your time to step up where others are slowing down, your time to dig deep for the final sprint, and your time to demonstrate mental strength. This is tenacity; the ability to keep going when others give up. This famous quote by Theodore Roosevelt rings true when I think about the final push to create your best work.

> *"The credit belongs to the man who is actually in the arena, whose face is marred by dust and sweat and blood; who strives valiantly; who errs, who comes short again and again, because there is no effort without error and shortcoming; but who does actually strive to do the deeds; who knows great enthusiasms, the great devotions; who spends himself in a worthy cause; who at the best knows in the end the triumph of high achievement, and who at the worst, if he fails, at least fails while daring greatly, so that his place shall never be with those cold and timid souls who neither know victory nor defeat."*[37]

CHAPTER 9

FINAL THOUGHTS

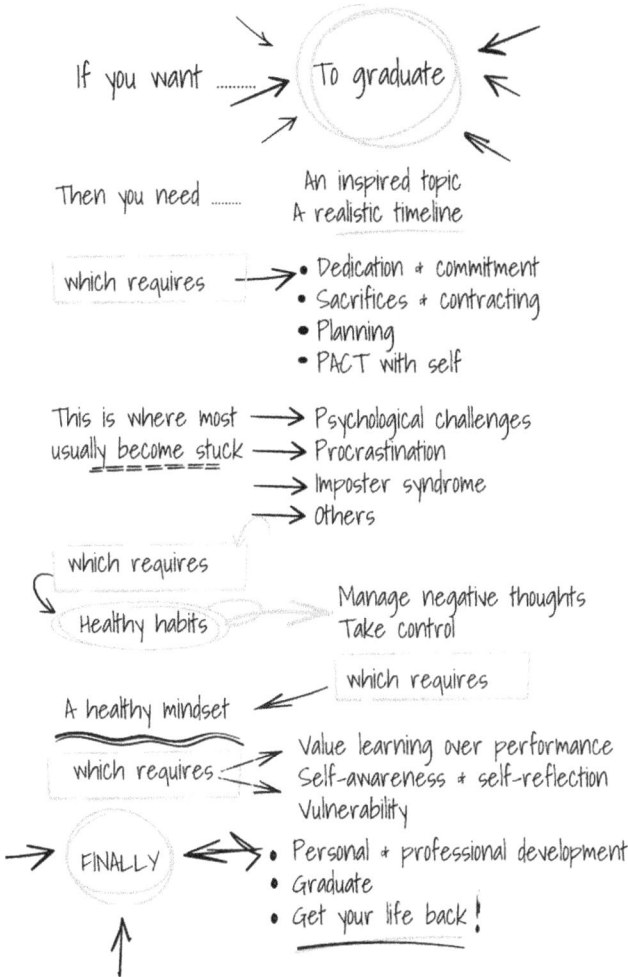

If you want .... → To graduate ←

Then you need ......
An inspired topic
A realistic timeline

which requires →
- Dedication & commitment
- Sacrifices & contracting
- Planning
- PACT with self

This is where most → Psychological challenges
usually become stuck → Procrastination
→ Imposter syndrome
→ Others

which requires

Healthy habits →
Manage negative thoughts
Take control

which requires

A healthy mindset ←

which requires →
Value learning over performance
Self-awareness & self-reflection
Vulnerability

FINALLY ←
- Personal & professional development
- Graduate
- Get your life back!

THE DALE METHOD

As you go through your thesis experience, you will reflect on your priority values and purpose. The decision to embark on this postgraduate journey suggests a commitment to learn, achieve and grow. The learning process will give you this opportunity for growth – academically, professionally and as a human being.

The task you have set yourself requires courage, strength, stamina, and above all, self-belief. You will learn to accept yourself in different ways and deepen your relationship with your life purpose. Brené Brown's academic research and work have taught me about vulnerability and shame. Suffering from a lack of self-confidence despite showing up as confident, successful and totally in charge is prevalent in many people. Not only postgraduate students but business leaders, entrepreneurs, famous people, and many more.

The prerequisites to success are perseverance, resilience and a positive attitude. The type of grit that keeps you going even when you're feeling alone and exhausted. My hope is that the advice available here will inspire motivation and confidence, and above all turn your experience into a rewarding, enjoyable and successful one.

APPENDIX 1

Learn to grow

None of this should be new to you, and I'm not the first person to notice the habits and attitudes of successful individuals. I understand you are bogged down with reading material, but if you're looking for some self-development tools, I highly recommend reading or listening to the following to deepen your understanding on these key behaviours.

- *Atomic Habits.* Learn the power of stacking habits as well as how small incremental changes can compound and alter a result to favour success.

- *Deep Work.* Learn how to build your levels of concentration to increase productivity.

- *Essentialism.* Learn how to say no to things so that you can stay focused on the work that really matters.

- *Keep your focus.* Forty thought-pieces on maintaining your top performance.

- *Why we sleep.* Gain insight into the critical importance of sleep and how it affects your brain and overall cognitive performance.

- Scan https://www.thethesiscoach.com where I've published several short articles on these topics.

REFERENCE LIST

Allen, D. (2019). *Success Is Easy: Shameless, No-nonsense Strategies to Win in Business.* California: Entrepreneur Press.

Arnot-Mulhern, S. (2020). *Keep your focus: 40 thought-pieces on maintaining your top performance.* Randburg, South Africa: KR Publishing.

Burkeman, O. (2021). *Four thousand weeks; time management for mortals.* New York: Farrar, Straus, and Giroux.

Chuong, H. (2017). *Paraphrasing strategies: 10 simple techniques for effective paraphrasing in 5 minutes or less.* Independently published.

Clear, J. (2018). *Atomic habits: tiny changes, remarkable results: an easy and proven way to build good habits and break bad ones.* London: Random House Business Books.

Collins, S. (n.d.). Goodread. Available from: https://www.goodreads.com/quotes/291217-it-takes-ten-times-as-long-to-put-yourself-back

Corey, G. (1996). *Theory and practice of counseling and psychotherapy.* Pacific Grove: Brooks/Cole Publishing Company.

DeMartini, J. (n.d.). The Demartini Value Determination Process. Available from: https://drdemartini.com/content/values/?tk=4662?utm_source=ga&utm_medium=ppc&utm_campaign=vd&utm_content=site-ext&gclid=CjwKCAjw4ayUBhA4EiwATWyBruY-MpzYeJQBaOMsqO1yFGrz5zZyiUspbS_XEnrsUIiCTGBSH2umehoCek4QAvD_BwE

Domar, A.D., & Dreher, H. (2000). *Self-nurture: Learning to care for yourself as effectively as you care for everyone else.* New York: Penguin Books.

Dweck, C. (n.d.). A Summary of Growth and Fixed Mindsets. Available from: https://fs.blog/carol-dweck-mindset/

Epictetus. (n.d.). Epictetus Quotes. Available from: https://www.goodreads.com/quotes/8670152-the-chief-task-in-life-is-simply-this-to-identify

Gaiman, N. (2021). 'You Can Sit There and Do Nothing…or You Could Do the Work.' Available from: https://anthony-moore.medium.com/you-can-sit-there-and-do-nothing-or-you-could-do-the-work-d881b224f566

Graff, G., & Birkenstein, C. (2006). *They Say I Say: the moves that matter in academic writing.* New York: W. W. Norton & Company, Inc.

Mate, G. (2018). *In the Realm of Hungry Ghosts: Close encounters with addiction.* London: Vermilion.

Maxwell, J. (1998). *The 21 Irrefutable Laws of Leadership.* Nashville, Tenn.: Thomas Nelson Publishers.

McKeown, G. (2020). *Essentialism: the disciplined pursuit of less*. New York: The Crown Publishing Group.

Miller, W.R., & Rollnick, S. (2002). *Motivational interviewing: preparing people for change*. New York: Guilford Press.

Moore, M., Jackson, E., & Tschannen-Moran, B. (2016). *Coaching psychology manual* (2nd ed). Philadelphia: Lippincott Williams & Wilkins.

Neenan, M. (2008). From cognitive behaviour therapy (CBT) to cognitive behaviour coaching (CBC). *Journal of Rational-Emotive & Cognitive-Behavior Therapy, 26*(1), 3-15.

Nelson, P. (1993). *There's a hole in my sidewalk: The romance of self-discovery*. Hillsboro, OR: Beyond Words Publishing.

Newport, C. 2016. *Deep work: Rules for focused success in a distracted world*. London: Piatkus, Brown Book Group.

Norcross, J. C., Krebs, P. M., & Prochaska, J. O. (2011). Stages of change. *Journal of Clinical Psychology, 67*(2), 143–154. http://doi.org/10.1002/jclp.20758

Peltier, B. (2009). *The psychology of executive coaching: Theory and application*. New York: Brunner-Routledge.

Peterson, J.B. (2018). *12 rules for life: An antidote to chaos*. Canada: Random House.

Petrocelli, J.V. (2002). *Processes and Stages of Change: Counseling With the Transtheoretical Model of Change*. Journal of Counseling & Development, 80(1), 22–30.

Prochaska, J.O., Wright, J.A., & Velicer, W.F. (2008). Evaluating theories of health behavior change: A hierarchy of criteria applied to the transtheoretical model. *Applied Psychology, 57*(4), 561–588. http://doi.org/10.1111/j.1464-0597.2008.00345.x

Prochaska, J.O. (1984). *Systems of psychotherapy: A transtheoretical analysis*. Homewood, IL: Dorsey Press.

Roosevelt, T. (n.d.). Theodore Roosevelt Quotes. Available from: https://www.goodreads.com/quotes/7-it-is-not-the-critic-who-counts-not-the-man

Smallwood, D. (2014). *Who says I'm an addict? A book for anyone who is partial to food, sex, booze or drugs*. London: Hay House UK Ltd.

Stevenson, S. (2016). *Sleep smarter. 21 essential strategies to sleep your way to a better body, better health, and bigger success*. New York: Rodale Books.

Endnotes

1   Clear, 2018, p27.
2   Graaf & Birkenstein, 2006.
3   Graaf & Birkenstein, 2006.
4   Maxwell, 1998.
5   Prochaska, 1984.
6   Clear, 2018.
7   Clear, 2018.
8   Clear, 2018.
9   Petrocelli, 2002.
10   Miller & Rollnick, 2002.
11   Norcross et al., 2011.
12   Prochaska et al., 2008.
13   Nelson, 1993.
14   Nelson, 1993, p2–3.
15   Clear, 2018, p21.
16   Gaiman, 2021.
17   Newport, 2016, p51.
18   Newport, 2016.
19   Petersen, 2018.
20   Petersen, 2018, p83.
21   Neenan, 2008.
22   Neenan, 2008.
23   Arnot, 2020, p9.
24   Smallwood, 2014, p5.
25   Mate, 2018.
26   Collins, n.d.
27   Stevens, 2016, p1.
28   Stevens, 2016.
29   Dweck, n.d.
30   Peltier, 2009.
31   Allen, 2019.
32   Burkeman, 2021.
33   McKeown, 2020.
34   DeMartini, n.d.
35   Moore, Jackson & Tschannen-Moran,
36   Epictetus, n.d.
37   Roosevelt, n.d.

INDEX

www.ingramcontent.com/pod-product-compliance
Lightning Source LLC
Chambersburg PA
CBHW072156090426
42740CB00012B/2283